Strictly for the Chickens

Frances Hamerstrom

Strictly for the Chickens

Illustrations by Elva Hamerstrom Paulson

The Iowa State University Press / Ames, Iowa

Most photos, unless otherwise indicated, by Frederick Hamerstrom.

Composed and printed by The Iowa State University Press, Ames, Iowa 50010

First edition, 1980

Library of Congress Cataloging in Publication Data

Hamerstrom, Frances, 1907–
    Strictly for the chickens.

    Bibliography: p.
    1. Greater prairie chicken. 2. Birds, Protection of—Wisconsin. 3. Hamerstrom, Frances, 1907– 4. Hamerstrom, Frederick. 5. Birds—Wisconsin. 6. Ornithologists—United States—Biography. I. Title.
QL696.G285H35   333.95′8′0922   80–19387
ISBN 0–8138–0800–6

CONTENTS

v

AUTHOR'S NOTE

Is this book true? It's as true as I could write it. Nothing has been changed to make it more plausible.

Among the many debts I have incurred are:

To two outstanding research chiefs of the Wisconsin Department of Natural Resources, Cyril Kabat and James B. Hale, who courageously fought for the prairie chickens and our long-term project.

To Dr. Ruth L. Hine for twenty-six years of editorial help and inspiration.

To about 7,000 "boomers" who helped by reading numbered bands on legs of chickens and brightened our lives for some twenty-five springs.

To a Lady named Luck who helped spring me from a cultured, but narrow, background into the wide, wide world of other real people—from other walks of life and opportunities that round out our beautiful world.

To the Prairie Chickens of Wisconsin who have just staged a population explosion.

F. H.

January 1, 1980

FOREWORD

ONCE UPON A TIME there was a beautiful young girl and a handsome young man, both from wealthy and cultured Boston families. They met at a Dartmouth house party, fell in love and were married. They did live happily ever after, but not in Boston. They chucked all the trappings of high society and moved to central Wisconsin, where they chose to live the lives of pioneers thrust against some of the worst winter weather in American history.

Those two young people were Frederick and Frances Hamerstrom. The reason for the dramatic change in their lifestyle has to do with the saving of a not-so-well-known game bird called the greater prairie chicken. Because of the Hamerstroms' dedication, energy, and knowledge over the last forty years, the greater prairie chicken in Wisconsin has been brought back from the brink of extinction.

However, *Strictly for the Chickens* is not a biological treatise on how the prairie chickens were saved. It is a collection of heart-warming and highly entertaining stories about two people and their love for each other and for a game bird in trouble.

I have known Fran and Fred Hamerstrom most of my life. I remember hearing about them more than thirty years ago when my parents drove from Pittsburgh to the Wisconsin marshlands to write an article about their work with prairie chickens. I vividly recall how excited Mom and Dad were when they got home to tell my sister and me all about the Hamerstroms. During the years that followed, I, too, have known the excitement of visiting the Hamerstroms. To see them at their best, one must be there in early spring. After receiving their final instructions and a few hours of sleep, you rise at 3 A.M. and are shown—in the dark—to an observation blind in the Buena Vista Marsh. Through a slit in the wall you thrill to one of the greatest sights in the world of natural history . . . the dancing of cock prairie chickens on their ancestral booming grounds. But everyone who is placed in a blind is expected to assist by recording pertinent data. The combination of seeing both the Hamerstroms and the prairie chickens in action at the same time is one of the great rewards of working in the field of wildlife.

For those who are not familiar with the bird, the prairie chicken is not a chicken at all, but a grouse. It is to the prairies what the ruffed grouse is to the forests. It is eighteen inches long, weighs about two pounds, is short-tailed and buffy-brown with barred underparts. It spends most of its time on the ground, but in the air the prairie chicken can outfly even a peregrine falcon in straight level flight.

By the late 1920s the historical habitat of the prairie chickens in the Middle West was being victimized by the same villain that claimed the heath hen a few years earlier—encroaching civilization and misunderstanding of its needs.

Much of the responsibility for saving this magnificent game bird fell to the biologists in Wisconsin who took the lead in prairie chicken research. A series of brilliant scientists named Gross, Schmidt, Grange, and finally, Hamerstrom documented the natural history of this glamorous, noisy, and colorful bird known to science as *Tympanuchus cupido pinnatus.*

Under the guidance of a professor at the University of Wisconsin who was none other than Aldo Leopold, the young Hamerstroms began their all-important research in the late 1930s.

Their work continues today. Not only are Dr. Frances Hamerstrom and Dr. Frederick Hamerstrom the recognized authorities on the greater prairie chicken, but they have also made significant contributions in the fields of European grouse, birds of prey, and accurate nature books for children.

I hope that this background on the Hamerstroms will give you even more enjoyment and appreciation of these two beautiful people as you read the *real* story of how Fran and her "Hammy" fought to save the prairie chickens in Wisconsin.

GEORGE H. HARRISON

Hubertus, Wisconsin

To the most fascinating man I ever met

Frederick Hamerstrom

And then there were none

I vividly remember the first time in my life when my courage failed me: May 12, 1916. The wind blew hot and dry. It roared through the treetops near the tennis courts at West Chop on Martha's Vineyard island. It was the day of the junior tennis tournaments. Older children were playing on one court and the little ones, including me, were playing on the other. The roaring wind was my friend; it threw the boy I was playing against off his game and I was winning.

The wind roared strong and dry that day. A few miles away a fire raged over some twenty square miles of the last stronghold of the heath hen, the prairie chicken of the East. The wind rose to gale proportions. Several hundred men and women, and I suppose even children, rallied to fight the fire. According to the *Vineyard Gazette,* May 18, 1916, "The buildings on the state heath hen reservation were saved by desperate work of the fire fighters. Some of the heath hen were burned—perhaps a tenth of the number of old birds—and all the eggs for this year's crop of young were destroyed. . . ."

There were roughly 2,000 heath hens in 1916 and the next year the population was down to about 175. It never recovered. In 1928 only three birds were reported and in 1932 the heath hen was declared extinct. I remember the wind roaring over the tennis courts.

And I remember a truck that veered off the road and drove right across the lawn to where we were. It was so sudden and peculiar that we all gathered around and the driver, an old fisherman, shouted, "Fire! The Great Plain's afire!" He pointed at the empty back of the truck, "We need help."

We—the city kids—stood perfectly still, gathered around the truck. I looked at the big boys, but nobody said a word. I tried to speak—to say I'd help—but no words came. And when the truck drove away empty, I was ashamed. The wind swept hot crackling fire over the nests and eggs of an endangered race; it roared in the treetops by the courts. We played tennis.

3

Perhaps the shame of that episode left its mark on my life. At any rate I learned so young about the impending doom of a species and later when I had grown up I helped to avert another doom. By a strange quirk of fate I have spent most of my life working with Frederick—my husband—to understand and preserve the greater prairie chicken whose ancestral home is in the prairies of the West. We have gotten up over and over again (actually about 1,044 times) before the chickens left their roosts, to learn their ways. We devised traps so we could catch them unharmed and band them to study individuals (and we kept our babies in prairie chicken traps instead of play pens). We invented a way to restrain a prairie chicken gently while it was being weighed (put in an old wool sock). We built blinds so that we and countless other observers could study behavior during the booming season, Booming is the fantastic mating display in spring, when the cocks blow up big orange air sacs on their necks and make sounds like low-pitched organ music.

We have fixed up and moved into four abandoned farm houses to be near the chickens.

I had thought of calling this book *The Things One Doesn't Say*. Not that these things are hush-hush. But what lies back of scientific work seldom shows in a technical paper or book: the viewpoints of the public, the adventures of the investigators, and the fascinating struggle to find out more.

Two worlds

The onset of the winter of 1935–1936 north of Necedah, Wisconsin, probably struck our widely scattered neighbors as normal: a bit more snow and colder than usual, but essentially normal. Frederick takes things more calmly, but for me each day glowed with the sense of wild adventure. Sailboat racing, riding in horse shows, tennis, dancing all night, and even what camping we had done had not prepared us for survival in central Wisconsin: nor for our first job in prairie chicken country.

The kitchen end of the abandoned farmhouse we rented for five dollars a month sagged away from the rest of the house and the opening was stuffed with rags and old quilts. We pulled out and burned all this rubbish and plastered the gap. I know now that the rags were better insulation than our plastering job, but our families and teachers had never taught us anything like this. I had, however, gleaned a useful hint from an unexpected source. My governess, who had tutored Sir John Parry's daughter Joan before coming to look after me until my sixteenth year, told me about a ghastly fright she once had. Admiral Parry and his entourage were in Tasmania; Fräulein was upon the toilet seat in the outhouse and a sailor opened the back to take out the buckets! I loved to hear her tell this story. It didn't seem proper and Fräulein's stories were seldom as risqué as this.

So one day when Frederick was not at home, I managed to find two buckets and place them on planks beneath the outhouse holes. I thought this was nicer and it gave me great satisfaction to get everything shipshape for the winter. But Tasmania has a milder climate than central Wisconsin: I had a surprise in store. Both buckets filled up with alarming rapidity. Again I waited until Frederick was away because he would have insisted that the outhouse was *his* job. I put on my boots and outdoor clothes and went out to empty the buckets by our dump heap. The contents were frozen solid! No amount of banging against trees would dislodge them.

Our woodpile was pitifully small so an outdoor fire was out of the question. I lit two burners on the kerosene stove to heat the buckets. From time to time I tested with a stick to see how the thawing was progressing, muttering wise sayings like: menial work is honorable, manual labor is not demeaning. At last I was able to empty the buckets, and in spite of the bitter cold, I aired the kitchen. Then I washed my face, my hands, my hair, my shirt, my trousers, and my socks.

One of our treasured possessions, an oval mirror with a gold patterned frame, hung in our living room. As though drawn by an invisible thread I went into the living room to look at myself. I looked at my face a long time, and then I spoke to it: *"Anyway, I'm me."*

It made me feel much better. I practiced court curtsies in front of the mirror for a while. Through no fault of my own I was born with a silver spoon in my mouth and my grandmothers had fully expected that I would be presented at court some day. Twelve years of dancing school and dancing masters had perfected my curtsies. Now the world of cities, of dancing, of theaters, and servants seemed thousands of miles away and eons behind me. Not for all the capitals in Europe and the wealth of the Indies would I give up what I had now: love, adventure, and public service in the unmapped wilds of central Wisconsin.

Frederick and I made the first real road map of part of central Wisconsin. Our instructions were: any trail you can travel by car is a road. The vastness of the area was staggering. Interlocking trails seemed to lead nowhere, but now and again led to a house rather like ours. We saw very few people. Finally, late one summer I saw my first American Indians. I'd been looking forward to this for a long time. They were in a sky blue Pierce-Arrow touring car and they all piled out of it and came eagerly toward me. The driver asked, "Say, can you tell us the way to town?" Later, I met and worked with Jimmy Blake, an Indian who slid silently through the brush and didn't get lost, who could walk right past our campfire without our noticing him, and who taught me much of the woodlore that I know today.

We tried to explain to our neighbors, to Indians, to everyone what we were doing and why: that this great region was to become public domain and that the wildlife would be managed so the sand-hill cranes (then rare) would trumpet over the marshes each spring, the prairie chickens would boom in the early mornings, the fur harvest would be planned, and the deer would be held down so they would not overbrowse their range. We tried to teach conservation.

One day we encountered two boys about sixteen and eighteen years old herding cattle. Frederick brought out his best one-syllable words and gave them a splendid explanation of game management. Both listened without a flicker of expression. At last one boy's lips moved a little as though he might be about to say something. Frederick paused expectantly, but the boy turned to me. He asked politely, "What good does it make to paint your lips for?" And again I was reminded of two worlds.

Flame velvet

Together, joyously, but not without trepidation, we had made the decision to burn our bridges behind us, cross the Rubicon, and take to a life as biologists in the wilderness. Such decisions are rather glorious, but somewhere, way in the back of my being was a small impish flame that gave me the impression that if we really wanted to, we could unmake our decision and go back to the old, easy, rather charming mode of life we had known before. In my case it was an episode, which now strikes me as rather silly, that doused that small flame—that odd little half hope that we might combine the old with the new. Thawing and emptying those two outhouse buckets brought me bang! awake! My interest in any wan hope of going back was as thoroughly extinguished as though an irreversible chemical reaction had taken place. Frederick's episode was yet to come and still bothers us both a bit.

My episode involved just me. And it seems odd to me now. Imagine a sensible woman in her mid-twenties getting so keyed up at cleaning an outhouse that she had to go stare at herself in a mirror afterwards and draw strength from past glories.

Now that I look back on it, I think what a blithering idiot I was to make such a fuss. And then I remember the way I was brought up: well-bred girls always wear hats and gloves when in the city, they wear gloves when cutting roses in the garden, and they make sure to wash their hands after patting the head of a dog.

I reckon that some women just naturally whistle when they have an unpleasant little job to do with their hands; others learn to whistle while getting it done neatly, and still others shrink delicately from such situations, convinced that they are the really true ladies. Frederick scolds me if I beat him to an unpleasant job, but he has never accused me of not being a lady. He simply announces, "You should have let me do that."

8

We cut our firewood with a two-man saw for the first time that winter, and the snow piled out of the sky and drifted until some of the drifts reached two-thirds up the telephone poles. Then the roads drifted shut and we subsisted on what we had in the house. Snowed in. We did our work daily, trekking on snowshoes to census game; we cut more firewood and learned to heat only one small room, the kitchen—and of course, only when we were there.

Day after day we counted flocks of prairie grouse and learned to distinguish between the dark bellies and square tails of the prairie chickens and the light bellies and pointed tails of the sharp-tailed grouse.

We counted quail too, and as the temperature kept dropping, the coveys got smaller and smaller. Finally, we, on snowshoes, were able to pick up emaciated starving quail that no longer could fly, or even run. Their breastbones stuck out in sharp fleshless keels and we gave a few of the thousands of quail a swifter death than the slow starvation that took the rest of them that winter.

We got "snow stupid." Outdoors, we were alert and awake, but all we wanted to do when we got home was to get warm, to sleep, to sit, or to eat. Quite often I fell sound asleep during supper with my head on the table next to my unfinished meal.

9

Our chores at dusk were always the same: start the fire in the kitchen (a room that went from 20° below zero to fairly comfortable in about half an hour), pump water, cook, eat, write up field notes, and crawl into bed.

Snow stupid, alone together, we were content. We spoke very little; it seemed that each knew what the other was thinking. Our vocabularies dwindled and unplanned sign language took over. There were good books in the house for "the long winter evenings." They stayed on the shelf unread. We were content.

Suddenly, late one afternoon, our chores multiplied. At first neither of us realized that just one change in our relatively smooth schedule could cost so many extra hours of work and use up so much energy. The pump froze.

The kitchen was just getting warm enough so I couldn't see my breath. I had taken off my mittens to chop apart some frozen meat for supper when Frederick burst into the house saying, "We need boiling water—lots of it."

Both of us filled the washtub and two buckets with snow. We set one on the wood stove and the others over the two burners of the kerosene stove. Snow melts *very* slowly and huge quantities of fluffy snow produce only about a glass of water.

I lit the two burners under the oven to thaw and cook some meat, but thawing meat seemed disloyal to the present emergency, so I filled the oven with pie plates filled with snow.

We ate some dried prunes and bread. From time to time we left the steaming kitchen to get more snow. Stars sparkled in the still black night and sporadically the ground cracked like a pistol shot as the frostline seeped lower. It was probably about 35° below zero.

Long past our bedtime we were ready to thaw the pump. Frederick jiggled the long pump handle and I poured boiling water into the little hole at the top. It didn't take long: in a moment or two we succeeded in filling the whole inside of the pump with solid ice. A collar of ice formed around the top of the pump and thick vermiform icicles exuded from the collar. There was still a little lukewarm water left. We stirred in some powdered milk, and drank what was left of what I believed to be the end of the great snow-melting episode.

But day after day we melted snow. Snowmelt for drinking, snowmelt for dishwashing, snowmelt for baths, snowmelt for washing clothes, and snowmelt for rinsing the soap out of them. We had to cut extra wood to keep a fire going strong, for kerosene was expensive and besides our supply was rather low.

At last help came. Two neighbor boys, Alex and Andrew, who had walked through the woods in autumn carrying us sacks of potatoes and a citron when we had first moved in, came by to see how we were doing. Andrew scratched his neck with his mitten and took a good look at our pump. "Got some rags an' some kerosene?"

Frederick produced a can of kerosene and I went to hunt up some rags. I poked about in odd, cold corners of the house and barn, but I had been taught that rags are filthy and had burned every single one. Then I rummaged among our clothes to see what could best be spared. By the light of a kerosene lamp, I unpacked our suitcases and boxes in the cold upstairs storeroom, and one by one I threw things to keep on the floor behind me.

There was my tweed suit, made for me by a Boston tailor—might need that again someday; the underwear from my trousseau had very little bulk, and I had a feeling that pure silk wouldn't burn very well anyway. There was a real find: a pair of flannelette pajamas. Each night we both wore two pairs of pajamas, two pairs of bedsocks, and mittens to bed. And pajamas were essential in daytime too—for field work. We wore them under our clothes because we didn't have money enough for warm winter underwear. With increasing desperation I emptied boxes, and my little pile of potential rags hardly grew at all: we needed everything.

At the bottom of one wooden box I came on a specially wrapped container, large and white and tied with narrow mauve ribbons. It was from Saks Fifth Avenue. In it was my flame-colored velvet evening dress. Flame-color that picked up the golden glints in my hair; the low, soft cowl neck that Frederick considered so becoming; and the full, floor-length skirt that had floated in undulating swirls as we danced together under crystal chandeliers. I would never wear it again. I hurried downstairs whistling and handed it to Andrew. His big hands felt the bulk of the material. He nodded and wrapped my dress around the pump. Alex poured kerosene, soaking the dress again and again. Then he reached in his shirt pocket for a match.

I went back into the kitchen and watched the flames leap high, almost as high as the branches of the jackpine by our back door. I looked at the men. Alex and Andrew, heavyset, with rough-hewn, strong features, warmed themselves by the fire, secure in a job well done. Frederick stood a little apart, aristocratic and elegant, even in his worn field clothes. I could see his fine black eyebrows and his small straight nose. He wasn't watching the flames. He watched my dress, and when it was gone he still looked at the pump. His face was inscrutable.

12

Be alone when you talk to yourself

By the time we knew how to catch a prairie chicken and how to thaw a pump, we felt ourselves more or less seasoned wildlifers. We had had our introduction to attitudes toward female biologists, and idealistic ideas from Washington, but we were to learn more about local politicians.

The first time we ever voted in a presidential election we voted *against* Franklin Delano Roosevelt although his resettlement program was our source of bread and butter. We drove to town and went into a cheerless building. Our names and addresses were recorded and then we stood in between some little partitions—each arranged in such a way that you could pull a small cotton curtain behind you and nobody could see what you were writing. Next, having checked off our presidential choice, we folded the ballot and put it in a slit in a rather large wooden box. We did not look to see whether or not the box was locked.

Frederick and I left our booths feeling rather noble. We had voted against Roosevelt and against our own personal interests as well. Arm in arm, we walked down the street feeling pleased with ourselves.

Presently we heard a man running behind us; he grabbed Frederick's arm. "You made a mistake!"

"A mistake?" Frederick inquired in mystification.

"Yes, you didn't put the 'X' in the right place. You didn't vote for Roosevelt!"

Frederick looked at the distraught town chairman, or whoever he was, and uttered just five words. They were final. "We did it on purpose."

Those who are distressed by government spending nowadays are plunged into a welter of confusion. We were not: the problems where we were covered only a measly 100,000 acres, and Frederick

13

had been told by the Resettlement Administration of the United States government that he was in charge of the whole Central Wisconsin Game Project: Necedah.

There was an office in town. He didn't spend much time in that faraway office, but on December 29, 1935, he was informed that he would have 500 men working under him in five days! He announced he would be in the office every day, including Saturday and Sunday, and that he would hire foremen.

Frederick had never directed more than two or three people in his life before and one of them had always been me. How to keep 500 men busy? Three of the foremen hired that day became leaders of special game projects and worked with us in the field. Frederick's instructions were to put thirty-man crews to work. This he did. Thirty-man crews were easier to transport in a truck, but he stubbornly kept those three foremen, not to direct others, but so that he could have his own research crew.

The workers were on the relief roll. They were hired whatever their capabilities were, but he could hire anyone he pleased as a foreman. When interviewing Bud Truax, one of his three foremen, Frederick discovered that Bud's father had a good job with the railroad, his brother was a school teacher, and Bud himself was far from destitute. But Bud's application stated he was on relief.

"How is it," Frederick asked gently, "that you are on relief?"

"Why I'm not on relief, sir." Bud was soft-spoken and blushed easily.

Frederick pushed Bud's application over to him. "Is that your signature?"

"Yes, sir."

"Didn't you *read* what you signed? This states you are on relief."

Bud shook his head sadly.

Frederick grabbed the application and went straight to the office manager. "There's been a mistake here. This man is not on relief."

Mr. Gaffney, a ruddy-faced, silver-haired politician, gave Frederick a broad wink. "That's all right. We'll let it go. We're helping *lots* of people."

As the months passed Frederick and Mr. Gaffney got into numerous disputes: over and over again one gave an order and the other countermanded it. Just as Frederick thought he had the office running smoothly, with the furniture where he wanted it and each girl working to the best of her abilities, Gaffney rearranged everything.

Frederick put Isobel, who was a marvel at typing technical papers, in a quiet corner where she could work without interruption. Mabel, who could neither type nor spell, was moved up front to answer the telephone and field questions, which she did very well. That was on Friday. On Monday Isobel's desk had been moved up front again.

Frederick sent Bill's crew out to repair the dike road and when Bill reported in, his crew had trimmed some Norway pines instead.

This type of thing went on daily for months and it is a credit to both men that unpleasantness was always kept below the boiling point. Frederick is always polite and almost always reasonable. Gaffney was an outstanding manipulator, as most good politicians are. The situation gradually became more and more impossible. One day after another merry little turmoil, Frederick said quietly, "After all, I'm in charge of this office."

Gaffney sputtered, *"What?"* He stomped to his desk and produced a document that clearly implied that he was in charge of the *whole* project. Frederick produced an almost identical document! Eventually a long-overdue directive from Washington clarified the division of duties: Frederick was to direct game management and specify the work to be done, and Gaffney was to run the office—to attend to the details of hiring and firing, time sheets, payrolls, and the like.

I had nothing to do with the big crews. Not all 500 men showed up, but there were hundreds and no equipment for them to work with. For months there were no shovels, no axes, no wheelbarrows. To keep them busy, William Schuenke invented something called "The Continuous Game Inventory." Lines of men walked through the woods and marshes counting flocks of prairie chickens, sharp-tailed grouse, quail, rabbits, and deer. Crews often got lost, and if they encountered me—a girl cruising the woods alone—they not infrequently had to ask just where they were. Later, after most of the men had gotten work elsewhere, or disappeared for one reason or another, crates of brand new equipment arrived—shiny new shovels, axes, and tools, some of which none of us could identify. The forester's shed was used to store them in.

So much for big crews. Frederick put me in charge of a crew! My position on this federal project was distinctly shaky because of my sex. We both felt fantastically lucky because Frederick had wangled an agreement—although he never could get it in writing—that I was to be permitted to work full time—without salary.

And now I was to have a crew! To be sure, my crew consisted only of two men: Bud, who blushed so easily, and Os, who carried a huge thermos bottle of coffee wrapped in a blue blanket wherever he went. I had never directed a crew before and was determined to do it well. Frederick brought them to the house, announcing, "We need owl pellets." Then he jumped into the car and drove off.

First, I told my crew, "Owls gulp much of their food down whole." I added, "As they can't digest bones very well they cough up pellets with fur or feathers outside and the bones are inside."

OS AND BUD

Bud leaned forward. "You mean that this comes out of their *mouths?* They are trying to. . . ."

I could see him trying to form the word "vomit" and quickly said, "Yes, we'll pick up all the pellets we can find and later we'll pull them apart to see what the owls have been eating."

Silence.

"The horned owl's pellets are about half the size of a cigar. They are grayish and you'll find them under pines and leafy oaks where the owls like to spend the day."

I cut off further discussion by getting out a map. It was marked off in square-mile sections. "I'll take this middle section. Bud can take the section to the east of mine, and Os can take the section to the west. Everybody will work his own section thoroughly and we'll meet at the truck about sundown."

Each of us carried a big paper bag to put the pellets in. I moseyed along from one likely looking roost to another finding none. Just outside my section to the west was a fine-looking stand of old pines, but they were in Os's section and it wouldn't be fair to tres-

16

pass. Shortly before noon I ran into a horned owl winter territory and knew I wouldn't come out of the woods with an empty bag. I ate my lunch of a cold meat sandwich and raisins and continued on my way. Then I hit the jackpot: countless pellets under one great white pine.

It is my custom, when alone, to talk to myself, or better still to argue with some distinguished character—real or imaginary. Furthermore, I tend to talk in French or German so I won't forget these languages. I had recently translated M. Guérin's splendid book on the food habits of the tawny owl. Of course, I had never met the author, nor did I have the slightest chance of ever doing so. There were, however, a few little points in his book with which I disagreed.

I dug among the pine needles, pulling forth more and more pellets, then shifting on my knees to a new spot, I dug for more. The flow of conversation never ceased, for M. Guérin was not there to answer or to interrupt. From time to time I paused to elaborate an especially telling point with both hands, and then again I stopped to indicate the size of a small pertinent detail, smiling with animation at my invisible listener.

It could be that a twig snapped or perhaps a shadow moved. Suddenly I had the distinct impression that I was not alone.

Bud had been standing behind me and apparently for some time. He blushed deeply, and so did I. He tried to speak, but it seemed to strike him as hopeless. I showed him my bag of pellets, but the scene he had just beheld rendered him incapable of recognizing what was in the bag.

Finally I pulled myself together to explain, but I started my explanation in French!

Clearly, it is important to impress one's crew *favorably* on the first day. It is now forty years later. Bud has had ample opportunity to forget a great many things, but he has never forgotten his first day on Fran Hamerstrom's crew.

17

The wildest animal

"What is the wildest animal you have ever handled?"

Sometimes I answer, "Bald eagles not only sink their talons into you, but bite as well. Golden eagles are strong and sometimes unpredictable. I've handled a fresh-caught adult badger, and been bitten by raccoons, dogs, cats, muskrats, mice, and an adder."

Most people seem to associate wildness with danger to themselves. Having handled a variety of wild and domestic animals since I was nine years old, my concern tends to be for the animal itself, rather than what it might do to me. By my definition of wildness, by far the wildest creature is the prairie chicken. No other animal that I have handled is so apt to fight constraint and injure itself. They are *wild!*

We have learned to handle hundreds of prairie chickens without injury and have passed on this information to others.

At first we thought that trapping prairie chickens for banding would be rather like pheasant trapping. Pheasants are phlegmatic creatures and walk calmly into funnel traps and feast on the grain within, seldom injuring themselves in a properly constructed trap.

We patterned our first prairie chicken traps after pheasant traps. They were six feet long, four feet wide, and three feet high.

We covered the traps with chicken wire and fashioned a funnel at each end. We placed the traps in a likely looking field, where the snow was well laced with chicken tracks. The bait was yellow ear corn. We arranged it with careful deliberation: some ears stuck up out of the snow, some lay carelessly on the snow inside the trap, and we knocked kernels from a few ears and spread them in a little path leading through the funnel entrance and right into the trap. This last stratagem served a double purpose in our minds because the partly denuded ears looked as though prairie chickens had already pecked kernels from them and surely the birds would gladly enter where other birds had already fed.

That night I dreamed of traps full of chickens, and as though Frederick suspected how high my hopes were, he tried to fend off disappointment. "We'll be very lucky to catch one or two."

But I knew: I just felt it in my bones that we were going to make a good catch. I was right. We got out of the car, put on our snowshoes, and set forth joyously. Even from a distance we could see that we had caught quite a lot more than one or two.

Joy turned to horror, to despair. The birds had thrashed and beaten their way all around the edges of the traps, they had poked their heads through the wire mesh, and some had torn the skin across their scalps, exposing bare skull. There was a blood line about nine inches above the snow all around each trap, and the snow was spattered with blood. It was somehow like coming upon an automobile accident suddenly. It looked awful.

I know now that it wasn't nearly as bad as it looked. Most of the injuries were superficial. The abrasions on the wings would have healed nicely by themselves, and all the head injuries needed was three to five stitches to bring the skin back together. There really isn't much of a trick to suturing a scalp cut. After all, the skin is there; it just has to be pulled back into place and sewed up. If the edges of the skin are dry, I moisten and loosen them with my tongue; if the skull is dry I get plenty of spit on it and then I am very careful to line up the edges of the wound when I put in the stitches. I minored in veterinary medicine at Iowa State College, but no one ever told me to use my own spit when the temperature was 20° below zero. My teachers did tell me that upon occasion it is best to operate promptly and on the spot.

On the spot was right there, miles from any town, and we weren't seasoned. We killed those chickens that looked hopeless and banded the rest and let them go.

19

It was a bad setback in our trapping attempts—just our first setback. The next one was equally unexpected.

Of course we hauled the traps home and pried off all the wire. Then we tried to get some netting to cover the traps. There was none to be found and no money to buy any. By sheer good fortune one of the books we had with us was my grandmother's *Encyclopedia of Embroidery*. I wonder now whether I actually supposed that I might have time for embroidery, or whether I brought it along for sentimental reasons. On page 397 there are explicit instructions for making netting, illustrated by a helpful line drawing.

FIG. 614. FIRST POSITION OF THE HANDS.

We found string. The local bank and especially the offices of the Resettlement Administration supplied rather a lot. We asked people for string and we helped ourselves to string out of wastebaskets. We knotted the pieces together and then we sat on our kitchen table evening after evening and made netting, circumventing the knots. Sometimes it occurred to me that a future Ph.D. candidate could better employ his time, but it didn't take a Ph.D. mentality to figure out that we'd better sit *on* the table rather than *at* it. The floor was so cold that even in heavy field boots our feet got numb near the floor. I knocked a cup of hot coffee over one day and took the coffee up with a knife. It was frozen solid before I could reach a mop.

We sat on the table and netted. It was peaceful: no TV, no radio, just the crackle of wood in the stove and, in February, great horned owls called on still nights.

Our string, coming from so many sources, also came in many colors: stout white butcher's twine, black and white twisted string, green string, yellow string, and quite a lot of red string because Christmas was not far behind us.

Because prairie chickens can distinguish between yellow corn and white corn (they prefer yellow), we correctly assumed they were not color-blind. But we were incorrect in assuming that they would shun bright-colored netting. Frederick bought some olive-drab dye and I dyed all the netting in our washtub. I followed the instructions on the package carefully. I boiled the netting in this dye bath and then I set it with a mordant. The recommended mordant was not very expensive: it was salt. Even after all our work we had only enough netting to cover two traps, but we set these out near the edge of a likely looking field. Again I dreamed of a big catch, and we looked forward to checking our traps. The next morning there were no birds in the traps. But the snow near both was fairly stamped down with a multitude of tracks, and fragments of our netting moved lightly in the morning air. It appeared that all the squirrels and all the rabbits and all the deer in the county had come to feast upon that precious salt.

Jack wants to shoot

In the 1930s the area north of Necedah was a sparsely settled and sometimes violent land, described by many as desolate. Shortly before we moved in, a game warden had been shot and the general feeling of the country was against law and order, especially as far as game laws were concerned. Whole families were able to subsist on a cash income of $150 a year. Most grazed their scrawny cattle on public land, canned quantities of wild berries and bracken fern, found bee trees for honey, and supplemented their diet with deer meat. I didn't like the story about the game warden and made a point of telling everyone that my husband was *not* a warden—he was a *game manager* and had nothing to do with making arrests.

Central Wisconsin was also a country where the conversational art of telling complicated lies was developed to a high degree. There were strict rules—the lies had to have at least a kernel of truth. The neighbors were kind to us and brought odd and useful presents like a kerosene can that didn't leak because they had soldered it for us, food, two window panes, a year-old copy of the *Woman's Home Companion,* and a huge roll of felt that the paper mill didn't need any more. (After I had converted the felt to hide our worst floor, I learned that ''everybody'' made clothes out of paper mill felt.)

Especially Alex and Andrew, who lived a couple of miles away, brought us stories and gave us advice. Some of the advice was bizarre and some of the stories were innocuous.

22

"You gotta keep pigeons to attract away the lightening. Look," Andrew added, "see this gash onna floor? That's where lightening hit oncet."

Alex said that this was the bedroom and that the previous occupants had had an axe, a shovel, and a plowshare leaning against the bed at the time the lightning struck, but they tried to get us to believe that it would never have happened with pigeons around.

"If a hoss dies, bury it under the barn door an' no more hosses'll die in that barn."

"There's monkeys breeding in the river bottom." We traced that story. Opossums had only just extended their range so far north and their long prehensile tails gave the boys a fine chance to test our gullibility. They must have been having a very good time at our expense, and I'm sure they considered us stupid and often ungracious. How was I to know that when a polite Pole comes to your house, it is his duty to refuse any food offered? He must show that he came for the pleasure of your company, and it's up to the host or hostess to make the same offer again after a short period of grace. I offered from our scanty supplies, and when they said, "No," I believed them! They waited for me to offer again and I let them down.

It took a long time to learn local etiquette and even longer to evaluate and decipher the rules of telling lies.

We were unprepared when Alex and Andrew arrived one day, sat down comfortably in our kitchen, and Andrew announced, "Everybody knows you're not a game warden." I breathed a sigh of relief. "They all know it's *her*." Both boys looked at me. "They know *she's* the game warden."

"And," he continued, "you went past Jack Becker's barn, didn't ya?"

I *had* gone fairly close to the barn of our nearest neighbor while following the tracks of a covey of quail.

"Jack Becker knows," Andrew continued sadly. "You saw that deer hangin' up in his barn, and both his son an' his son-in-law had to leave out for Chicago."

"I never saw a deer in that barn!"

"Don't make no good to say that. Jack says as soon as he gets the chanct he's goin' to shoot Fred there."

Why Frederick? Either way it wasn't very pleasant. We made a few inquiries, "Have Jack Becker's son and son-in-law gone to Chicago?"

"Yes, two days ago."

I asked in the hardware store, "What's Jack Becker like?"

"He's all right . . . pays his bills, an' a good farmer. I

wouldn't want to cross him though . . . quick-tempered.''

"Has he got a gun?''

" 'Course he's got a gun.''

In the evening Frederick announced, "I'm going over to see Jack Becker.''

"And I'm coming too.''

"No, I'm going alone.''

"Please, darling, let me come too. Ladies have a softening influence.''

"I have made up my mind to go *alone.*''

"I'll wear a skirt—my green tweed skirt.''

"Fran, the matter is settled. I'm going alone and on foot.''

"But he wants to shoot *you,* not me!''

We argued far into the night. Breakfast was a quiet, miserable meal. Then Frederick put on his jacket and started for the Beckers' house. It was the only farm in sight of ours in that lonely country, and it was half a mile away.

I took our binoculars out of the case and went upstairs. Kneeling on the floor by an open window, I watched Frederick walk. His arms were swinging freely to show clearly that he was not armed.

We had agreed on one thing: walking was safer than appearing suddenly in a car, but now I couldn't help feeling that a car might have given some protection.

I watched the figure of the man I loved getting smaller and smaller, fearing that at any moment it would suddenly lie crumpled on the road. Time stretched like an enormous elastic—toward the breaking point of eternity.

I heard no shot and thought, but wasn't absolutely sure, that he had made it to the house safely. One thing I knew for certain: there are people around here who have shot a game warden. The only *fact* I had didn't make waiting any more reassuring.

Frederick came back down that long road alive. His account of what had happened was somewhat bewildering. "Jack Becker just laughed and laughed. He said, 'There wan't a word of truth in it— our boys didn't light out. They went to Chicago looking for jobs.' "

We became fond of Jack Becker. He had a job somewhere and managed to farm too. When corn-planting time came, he rode his tractor by moonlight and sang above the roar of the tractor. His songs were like a paean of praise to the world and the stars. We could hear his magnificent baritone when we were lying in bed. It was the voice of the man who didn't shoot Frederick.

The next year we were graduate students and lived near the suburbs of Madison, far from the mellow sound of booming prairie chickens and far from Jack Becker—singing on his tractor beneath the light of the moon.

But it's already done

Aldo Leopold was known by many of his students simply as "The Professor," as though there were no other professors on the University of Wisconsin campus. His office in 1938 was a small, badly lit room in the basement of the Old Soils Building. To enter it one passed through a sort of vestibule, used by the campus gardener as a potting shed. The potting shed was also the only "office" of The Professor's six graduate students. We kept a bannister brush hidden under the big table we used for making graphs, preparing specimens, and studying, so we could brush away begonia leaves, wet earth, and the fragments of flower pots that the gardener left behind.

Leonard Wing, one of the students, refused to work in the potting shed and tried to get the rest of us to keep it picked up so the entrance to The Professor's office would make a good impression. Late one afternoon, Wing, his dark eyes sparkling with suppressed excitement, whispered, "I've found a whole empty building on the campus. We are going to move The Professor. Bring your car at 8:00; it will be dark by then. You tell Hawkins, and I'll tell Wade."

We met at 8:00. Wing said, "I've found two wheelbarrows. Let's get the top of the Hamerstroms' car down right away; the big

26

things go on the car. I'll keep an eye out for the night watchman and the campus cops. If you hear the call of a barred owl, it's the signal: watch out. . . . And you, Hawkins, take off that white sweater. It shows a mile away.''

I hung the sweater over Leopold's desk lamp so passersby would be less apt to see what we were up to. We packed and moved all the books, all the reprints, all the maps, the duck decoys, and the furniture into a roomy empty building that had once been a dwelling. We moved everything and then, to convert the whole ground floor into Leopold's possession and fill the place up, we moved tables and chairs and bookcases from our own quarters and arranged them to ''occupy'' as many rooms as possible. As a final touch I picked some flowers from the campus gardens and put them in a mason jar on Leopold's desk.

Exhausted and somewhat grubby, we waited for Leopold's arrival the next morning. The Professor came down the path at a brisk pace. Leonard Wing, whose sense of the dramatic far surpasses mine, announced, '''Your office isn't here any more. Follow me.''

Wing led the way to 424 University Farm Place. He threw the front door open and announced, ''This room will be for seminars. It has a fireplace for winter seminars and it can hold forty people.''

Wing moved to the adjoining room. ''Your office!'' Sunlight poured in through big bay windows. All the books were in position on shelves that left room for more, and Leopold's pipe rested on the ashtray on his desk.

Wing let Leopold take it all in for a moment or two and then announced, ''There's more. This room is for graduate students. It needs more desks.''

He moved us on to the former kitchen. "This is the laboratory, It needs painting. We'll do that this afternoon."

Then he led the way to the pantry. "This is the darkroom. We'll paint it black. It has running water too."

Finally, he opened a door leading to a room almost as big as The Professor's former office. "We could use this for storage, and there is plenty of storage space in the basement too."

Leopold asked, "How did this come about?"

Wing's deep voice answered pompously, "The other office was not suitable for you."

The rest of us explained how we had managed the move with two wheelbarrows and one car "between two days."

Leopold sat on the edge of his chair and telephoned the authorities. We could hear only his end of the conversation. "You say that the building has already been assigned to another department? . . .

"Yes, I understand perfectly. What I'm trying to explain is not that I wish to move my office. It's already *done* . . . !

"No, just the ground floor. The whole ground floor." . . .

At last Leopold settled back in his desk chair, reached for his pipe, and lit it slowly. He didn't need to say a word. He was smiling and so were we. In those days not everybody knew that Aldo Leopold was a great man, but his students did.

"424 University Farm Place" was the address of Leopold's department for the rest of his life.

ALDO LEOPOLD

And sometimes, when I hear a barred owl call, I remember that night and the dread with which we listened for footsteps, police whistles, and for the warning that never came.

A letter from my mother-in-law

When Aldo Leopold assigned us both to work on prairie chickens, we could hardly believe our good fortune. I knew that Frederick would be accepted, but I never graduated from high school, and flunked out of Smith College in my sophomore year. To be sure, my scholastic record shot up after my marriage. I straightened out, graduated from Iowa State College, and even received a prize for the woman most likely to succeed in research. To work with Frederick as a team, rather than as a tag-along wife, I needed a chance to work for my Master's degree. Leopold never held my sex, nor my early scholastic record, against me.

And now we were about to head for our first field assignment on prairie chickens. Leopold arranged for us to move into a farmhouse in Waushara County. Clyde Terrill, the kindly owner, said, "Tell your students they don't have to pay rent. There are some broken windows upstairs; I hope they'll fix them. And I left some food up there once. Tell them they can eat it." He added, "I wish they'd paper the kitchen too." It was plain that—someday—he hoped to come back to a ramshackle old building that he had named "Paradise Found."

Frederick had a toothache.

He was cutting a wisdom tooth. I drove the last part of the way so he could hold his scarf against his jaw. We bumped through snowdrifts and at last the headlights picked up our new home. It was New Year's Eve, but for a fleeting moment I wondered whatever had possessed us to come straight from a party to move into a strange house after dark—and in city clothes. I could see the rusted screen of the front porch flapping in the wind. Frederick was crouched low holding his cheek. "You just stay in the car. I'll go in and get the house warm."

The key, we had been informed, was under a rock by the front door; in high heels I fumbled around in the snow, which was getting deeper by the minute, to find rocks. There were several—all frozen down. I let quite a blast of cold air into the car looking for the jack handle.

"Want me to help you?"

"No, I can do it. You just sit there."

Using a chunk of stovewood from the shed back of the house as a fulcrum, I tried to pry the rocks up. It was hopeless; they might as well have been set in cement.

Returning the jack handle to the car, I shouted, "I'll have to break in."

Frederick nodded without answering, but in a few minutes he joined me and together, without splintering too much wood, we jimmied the door open. I'm sure that if he hadn't had a great deal of self-control he would have been uttering little moans of pain. It didn't take much persuasion to get him back in the car to wait for the promised warm house.

I built a fire in the kitchen stove. All it did was belch smoke, so I had to open the doors and windows to let the smoke out. Next I tried the living room stove, an ornate heater with isinglass windows. The result was the same. Coughing and with stinging eyes, I aired the house thoroughly. There was a kerosene cook stove. We would have to make do with that. There were numerous cans that might have held kerosene; they were all empty, even the one with a frozen potato stuck over its snout.

Dejected and thoroughly chilled, I went out to the car. "Darling, do you think we can make it back to that last town? We have to buy some kerosene."

"We can try."

The drifts were piling up, but we made it back with a big can of kerosene. We lit the stove for a few minutes to warm up our hands. Then we felt our way up the narrow stairway and found a pile of quilts. Acorns tumbled out when we lifted them, and they smelled like mice. But we put the pungent quilts on a creaky bed and crawled between them. Slowly, slowly, the aching cold left our bones and we were warm. The next morning frost tipped Frederick's eyelashes. They were long and black and curved and frost tipped every lash. He smiled in his sleep and I knew the toothache was gone. At last he stirred and woke up.

We dressed quickly. I had to get back into my finery because my field clothes were still in the car, but Frederick soon produced the duffle bags so I could change in the icy kitchen.

Again smoke belched from the stove. Frederick adjusted the doors and the damper and tried all the tricks he knew to get a fire started. I tapped the stovepipe with a high-heeled shoe. We fought that stove with all the skill we had. Suddenly the smoke went up the chimney instead of out into the kitchen; the fire caught and crackled.

The house was full of food to augment our supplies: flour, prunes, raisins, sugar, syrup, pancake mixes, tea, coffee, dried milk, and unidentified pastes and mixtures. Only the coffee was labeled correctly. The flour was in a huge cookie can; cookies, raisins, prunes, and some mouldy bacon emerged from a fishing tackle box; I didn't find the jams and jellies for a long time. They were stored in milk bottles inside two big potato-chip cans marked ''Machine Oil.'' The remains of a package of cornflakes contained more mouse and squirrel droppings than cereal. We, too, soon learned to protect all food from marauding rodents.

Daily we explored the vicinity of our house on snowshoes looking for prairie chickens, and we finally found a few tracks in a rye field where the wind had exposed pigeon grass and ragweed. Then we asked our neighbor John, where we could find chickens.

''They's went . . . all went . . . used ta be some 'round here . . . they's went.''

Then he gave us the local news. It was said that Charlie Pratt was going to put in electricity! ''And you know what Pete did?'' Pete was our neighbor on the other side and we hadn't met him yet. ''Pete found an electric bulb onna dump an' he clumb the phone pole to hook it in, but he never got no yard light. He got nothing!'' John laughed hugely and offered us a drink.

We drank some stinging whiskey out of big white cups and took our leave. We headed for Pete's. There *was* an electric light bulb, fastened in some mysterious manner to the phone pole nearest Pete's house, and we didn't expect to learn much.

Pete may not have known much about electricity, but he knew where the chickens were. ''There's corn on the marsh,'' he waved his arm expansively toward the west. ''Too dry here, but the corn on the marsh grew good an' that's where the chickens are.''

He was right. We never saw any chicken tracks near our house again, so we hauled our traps to the Leola Marsh miles away and made some pretty good catches.

Our house was in the hills. They weren't big hills. Chunks of ice had become embedded in the moraine left by the last glacier and, when the climate became warmer the ice melted, leaving innumerable small ponds surrounded by hills. It was as though the

31

landscape had been designed by some devil to catch snow and plug up the roads in the year of our Lord, 1939. The winter landscape took on an unreal quality. The tops of telephone poles looked like fence-posts in the drifts. We never met anyone who had a telephone and I wondered where the poles led, tall on the hilltops and short in the valleys. Finally, we were snowed in with no way to get to the marsh where the prairie chickens were, some seven miles away.

The mailman came by our house. He had invented a *snow-mobile!* And this was almost surely the first snowmobile in the state of Wisconsin. This contraption had proved untrustworthy and was soon replaced by a factory model with six back wheels—three on each side—and runners in front. He romped across the top of the drifts followed by an enormous whirl of flying snow. The first time he came by, we thought the road must be open again; a machine that rode on top of the snow was beyond our imagination.

The snowmobile let us know that the road was still unplowed, and if the whirling cascade subsided at the end of our drive, we knew that the mailman had stopped and that there was something in the box for us. We rarely received mail; we had no bills to pay by mail, and no one consulted us professionally.

Our mothers kept writing us. Frederick's mother wrote me, I remember: when entertaining at luncheon use doilies instead of a tablecloth. It happened that I read the letter when sitting at our dining table. The decor consisted of a battered kerosene can and funnel; a lamp with a smokey chimney; an axe, saw, and hammer; two recent copies of the *Journal of Wildlife Management;* and a partly consumed can of sardines. The table was covered with patterned oilcloth; the pattern consisted of flowers in pots, and the cloth was cracked. . . . "Use doilies. . . ."

"And remember, dear," (she advised me on various matters as long as she lived) "to have your mink coat lined. It's just wrong to wear it the way you do."

I paused for a moment to recall an evening in New York and the face of the head waiter in the Stork Club. Even when I was a debutante I had made my own mink coat from an old one of my mother's, plus furs rescued from trunks in my parents' attic and road-killed mink that I had skinned and tanned myself. It was floor length, and its voluminous folds moved with grace when I walked because I had refused to line it. The inside of the coat consisted of the undersides of mink skins neatly sewn together. Some of the furrier's skins had little punch marks for coding the color and grade, a few of mine showed bite marks at the back of the necks of some females—wounds inflicted by the rough and tumble matings of big males with small females—and some of my hides were discolored.

Anyone who has been a fashion model and worked the East Coast circuit from Boston to Palm Beach well knows what sort of an impression her clothes are making. My escort and I had swept into the Stork Club slowly. No one needed to tell me that heads were turning. The head waiter, with a little nod to my escort—so to speak, asking permission— seated me and lifted my coat with slow dexterity from my bare shoulders. As he exposed the inside, putting it over the back of my chair, I heard something between a gasp and a wheeze. For a moment his aplomb had been shaken.

Now I had forgotten my mink coat and the mousy quilts had not been warm enough last night. I dug around in our boxes and found it. I spread it skin side down on our bed. It looked just beautiful.

Then I hurried down to the warmth of the kitchen, pried a couple of sardines out of the can with my fingers, and nibbled on them while continuing to read Mrs. Hamerstrom's letter.

"Frederick writes that you are living in a little wooden farmhouse. Window boxes are very attractive, dear Fran—window boxes abloom with geraniums and petunias—and often set a small house apart and give it a pleasant cottage look.

"And remember, dear, don't spoil Frederick. There are times to be firm."

Communicating with my mother-in-law was always something of a challenge.

"Dear Mrs. Hamerstrom,

"Thank you for your nice letter and for reminding me of my mink coat. Our house would seem small to you, but it is just right for us. It has three bedrooms, a living room, a kitchen, a well-stocked pantry, and a woodshed. It is pleasant to have the woodshed attached to the house; we never have to bother with wet wood and sit by a snug, cozy fire every evening after the day's work is done.

"Our house is nestled amongst exquisite wild pine trees. It has beautiful simple lines and the well-weathered wood fits beautifully into the landscape, which is somewhat hilly.

"So far we have not entertained here."

I pried the last sardine out of the can and drank the oil (those who have worked outdoors in cold climates know that the craving for fat and oil in the diet is intense, but I didn't think I'd tell her that).

Then I came to the part about not spoiling Frederick and I wrote exactly what I believe. "I have every intention of spoiling Frederick." To soften it a little, I added, "Men are to be spoiled."

We both loved Frederick, but we saw him with different eyes.

Geraniums . . .
red comforters . . . sleep

We thought it was impossible to snowshoe seven miles and back to tend our traps, but we were mistaken. At that time we had no real feel for prairie chicken trapping and set two or three traps out wherever we saw some tracks. Instead of waiting until a flock of chickens had almost exhausted a food supply and then moving in with a couple of dozen traps, we spread our trapline over many, many miles. Over and over again, we unset all our traps, lest an oncoming storm block the roads. Prairie chickens can probably spend a day or two burrowed under the snow without food, but we weren't taking any chances of finding dead birds in our sets. We checked each trap two, or even three, times a day.

STUCK . . . AND AGAIN

We had no radio, no news of the outside world, and no weather reports. We had to take some chances on the weather, or we wouldn't have caught any chickens at all. Each time we holed up, snowed in at home, we savored the comfort and solitude. Then when the plow got through, we drove to the marsh and had to find our unset traps and dig them out. Some were completely covered by drifting snow.

Once, in February, we failed as weather prophets. We drove home to a warm supper and creature comforts after a nice catch and careful baiting of all our traps. The next morning the roads were blocked solid!

I fried some meat, sliced some bread, and stuffed some sandwiches into our pockets. We ate a hearty breakfast and set out for the Leola Marsh. Our nearest traps were seven miles away, and the weather was a bit nippy for outdoor recreation.

Frederick laid out a plan: I was to unset the traps on the east side of the marsh, and he would take the west. Each knew exactly where the other was going and in what order we would unset the stations. Whoever got through first was to continue until we met. We met just before dark about nine miles from home. Scarves wrapped around our faces had saved them from frostbite, but the wind, if anything, had picked up.

We could see the dim light from a farmhouse lamp and headed for it and asked if we could come in and get warm. Mrs. Strattinger laid out a lavish supper for us, and Mr. Strattinger asked, "Where's your car?"

"Over at Clyde Terrill's. That's where we're living now."

"Well," he said, "you're going to spend the night right here."

Mrs. Strattinger took us upstairs to a room with geraniums on the window sill. She piled warm, red, feather comforters on the bed. It was just lovely, but neither of us can remember the room very well. It was like a moment on the TV screen when one button is pushed right after the next. Geraniums . . . red comforters . . . sleep.

She called us early the next morning, gave us a good breakfast, and we snowshoed home. The back door of the kitchen had blown open and I looked at the thermometer: it was 20° below zero in the kitchen.

Every house has something special. Clyde's, to be sure, had a back door that blew open in winter, but there were unexpected delights. There was a lake for swimming and for watching geese swing past dark oak woods to alight on the water. The lake was handy too. In summer I took a washboard to the beach and scrubbed the laundry clean. Then I rinsed the sheets by rushing along the shallows, avoiding the rocking grebe nests, and when I paused for breath, the

35

wild laughter of the loons echoed around me. There was an organ in that old house too. It was out of tune; but when Frederick was gone, I sometimes played *Oh dem Golden Slippers* or *Lavender's Blue* as loud as I could. And pasque flowers bloomed not far away.

Frederick reached a conclusion that I had almost arrived at by myself. "We're going to have to move. It's just too chancy trying to trap from way out here."

"Too chancy." Yes, it was too chancy to stay in this wonderful house. The chickens might hurt themselves—or even die—if we couldn't get to our traps regularly. The decision to move was made; but the chickens would be booming soon, and we had our hands full.

Anyway, we wouldn't be leaving till summer.

The open room

When spring came, visitors arrived to watch the prairie chickens. We hastily built more blinds and warned everyone to bring his own bedding. The help of volunteers augmented by our own industrious efforts made it possible to read the band numbers of many of the booming cocks.

Most of the visitors liked our warm untidy kitchen and rural setting, but one woman furtively wiped her silverware with a towel as though we hadn't washed the dishes, and looked at each chair before she sat down as though she might find a worm on the seat. When she found that we were moving soon, she took me aside and in a voice pent up with emotion, said, "I'm very glad for you."

Fortunately she didn't come to our next house. We never saw her again.

We found our next house by chance. Bill Feeney, a distinguished falconer and biologist, was with us. He had come to look our marsh over with us to see whether it would be any good for hunting with his birds. On our way home, out of curiosity, Frederick drove down a long, unused driveway and there was an old, old house with beautiful lines, and cut off from the rest of the world. We explored it. Most of the windows were still in and some of the floors were sound. But the roof leaked over the west end of the house, and one wall teetered in an inconsequential manner like a set on the stage.

The living room looked out on an ancient walnut plantation, tall elms framed the house, and mammoth white pines grew in the woodlot and along the driveway. We found out later that Walter Ware, the pioneer who built the house, had planted the pines by digging up frozen "root balls" and pulling them home on a sled with a team of oxen. It was Wisconsin's first pine plantation.

"This is it. We're going to live here."

Feeney had knocked about in the jingweeds and had undoubtedly spent some time in some pretty awful shacks in the backwoods. Sure that we were going to come to our senses, he simply said, "It must have been a nice place."

Feeney came to look for us in the autumn, knowing that we were living somewhere up in the chicken country. It took him a long time to find us, because he really hadn't believed for a moment that we seriously considered moving into *that* house.

Aldo Leopold was with us the first night we slept under the leaky roof. It rained and water beat on the windows and broken shingles outside and dripped through the roof into containers indoors. We set up a bed for him in the living room under the sound part of the roof, and set ours up in the kitchen. Pots, pans, and bowls filled up from time to time, and one large pan on the foot of our bed kept the water from drenching our bedclothes.

The next morning Aldo helped me dig a new hole for the outhouse. We dug through water-washed sand and hit a darkened layer.

"Must have been timber then and fires too. Drift sand can blow and build up fast, so we can't date it very well."

As we dug deeper and deeper, Aldo speculated on the ancient history of Glacial Lake Wisconsin, and I began to sense why the Leola Marsh had become one of the remaining strongholds for the prairie chickens. The glacial lake bed was colder than the surrounding country—too cold for many kinds of farming—so there were vast expanses of pasture and hay.

After about an hour of digging together, Aldo commented, "Interesting, isn't it? People make outhouses and such much bigger than they need to be." We agreed.

Aided by friends from the university, Frederick and I rebuilt that farmhouse. It is my impression that the roof was shingled by more Ph.D.'s than any roof in history.

We tore down the wobbly wall of our future bedroom—at that time we just called it "the open room."

When Aldo commented on the water-washed sand from the glacial lake bed, we had both rolled the smooth surfaces between our fingers. Neither Frederick nor I knew anything about mortar. We rebuilt the foundation along the north end of the open room. It was an enormous undertaking; we bashed apart the old rocks and mixed up mortar from the sandpile by the outhouse. Frederick wielded a borrowed trowel, set each rock in mortar, and used a spirit level to get the top straight. We went to bed exhausted, but very pleased with ourselves.

The next day it was plain that something had gone very, very wrong. Mortar poured in little trickles from between the rocks; it was dry, but we could pry any part of the foundation apart with our hands. Frederick asked, "Do you still have the bag this stuff came in?"

I had torn it up for lighting fires and stuffed it back of the woodbox. As we never subscribed to newspapers, each bit of paper was precious. I helped piece the torn edges together and Frederick reread the instructions. As I had suspected, the piecing together was a waste of time. Unlike me, he can read complicated instructions once and then *follow* them. He had followed them exactly.

The failure of the mortar could be a serious blow to our pocket book. We had $50 a month between us and had to run a car, and a trapline, and get to Madison 100 miles away for seminars, and eat—without any expense money. Frederick suggested he take the whole foundation down and that I go to town for more cement. The division of labor was well planned. Unlike Frederick, who is far too polite to argue, I can put up a good fight if anyone has sold us defective merchandise. By the time I had driven five miles over a bumpy road to the lumberyard, my righteous indignation was at perfect pitch. I never rehearse what I'm going to say; I just get in the right mood.

"The cement you sold my husband is worthless."

An old man peered at me over his bifocals. "Worthless? You mean it was caked?" He sounded incredulous.

"No, it was not caked. It just comes apart."

He sat back in his chair and looked at me through his glasses. "You fixing up the old Walter Ware place?" he asked conversationally.

"Yes." *I* wanted to be asking the questions, and matters were getting out of hand. "We are rebuilding a foundation and we need some good cement. There is something wrong with what you sold us."

"Where'd you get your sand?"

I longed to tell him it was none of his business, but instead, blushing violently, I stammered, "I got it from near the outhouse."

"Sand out that way is round. You've got to get your sand in the hills."

"In the hills?"

The old man rolled imaginary sand between his big knuckled fingers. He shook his head sadly, deploring my ignorance. "Sand in the hills is sharp-pointed and the cement will hold. Tell you what I'll do." He eased himself out of his chair and stepped out on the loading platform. "See, you go north two miles and west one mile, that's Manzer's Corners. You get your sand there. You got bags to put it in?"

I shook my head.

"Tell you what I'll do. I'll *give* you some bags."

Paying for cement a second time bothered me and almost emptied my purse, but I couldn't help protesting when he dumped a big armful of bags into the car. "I won't need all those!"

That old man didn't say anything. He just looked at me and somehow he managed to make me feel stupid.

Other people had been digging at Manzer's Corners. I pulled the shovel out of the back of the car and filled two bags in no time at all, opened the car door ready to put them in, and found I couldn't move them! Feeling an awful fool, I dumped most of the sand back on the ground and filled every bag up just a little so I could lift it.

Frederick had the foundation apart and the rocks washed clean when I got back.

"Darling, I had to pay for the cement!" In my own eyes I'd lost face, but I excused myself. "It was really only reasonable. The cement was all right; it was just that we used round, water-washed sand. Everybody goes to the terminal moraine to get sand for mortar."

Frederick was amazed. "Is *that* what the man at the lumberyard told you?"

"No, Aldo told me part of it, and I put two and two together."

"Did you get the potatoes?"

"I didn't have enough money," and then I added softly, "in my purse." That "in my purse" didn't fool either of us. A 100-pound sack of potatoes cost a dollar, but we didn't have a dollar anywhere.

"I hope there'll be some cement left so I can fix the chimney."

There was. I pulled every loose brick off the crumbling chimney, cleaned it, and mortared it back in place. It was almost dark when I

40

finished. Then I heard a screech owl calling. Herb Stoddard, the ornithologist, had just been up to spend a few days with us and had taught us how to call screech owls. You lie on your back and get a lot of spit ready; then you whistle low and falling and the spit rolls on your tongue trilling like an owl. I lay next to my rebuilt chimney and called. Before I could call again, a screech owl lit on the peak of the roof next to me.

The evolution of the chicken blind

Nowadays bird watchers—especially prairie chicken watchers—
sit comfortably in four- by four-foot cubes, or even bigger blinds.
Some actually bring their own dome-shaped blinds and can zip windows and camera ports open and shut at will.

After a heroic morning sitting in a blind watching prairie chickens, the normal man complains, "Cramped, I was—my teeth chattered—couldn't stand up—wind howled. . . ." I suppose hundreds have returned to the warmth of our big stove and complained
in many a picturesque manner. People like to tell me their troubles
so they tended to complain to *me,* and I gradually developed a series
of small, soothing mumbled phrases: "Must have been beastly
. . . um . . . what a pity . . . um."

I could have told them a thing or two. I could have told them about the booming ground that was so wild that the chickens refused to accept any sort of blind and I had to lie in a ditch—without *any* shelter—in the dark and wait for daylight and then wait again, without moving a muscle, head down in last year's pigeon grass, until my ears told me that the hens had finally flown away and at last it was time to jump up and count the cocks.

Later Frederick would ask, "You say you flushed *eleven* cocks? Are you sure the hens had all gone?"

"Yes, the 'ladies present call' stopped at 7:16 and then I waited about five minutes. I flushed cocks only and got the count."

"That booming ground wastes a lot of time." Frederick shook his head sadly, "Took all morning for you to get just one count."

All morning with my head in last year's pigeon grass, but it would never have occurred to me to answer, "Cramped . . . lying in that ditch head down . . . the wind blew the back of my jacket up . . . my feet are still numb."

Year after year we had to check that booming ground without using a blind. When I think back to our earliest blinds, I realize that some of them were almost as bad as having no blind at all.

Our first blind and our approach to the art of watching prairie chickens was incredibly naive. The game warden told us where to put the blind, and in March 1939 we set up a folding card table on a little knoll on the Leola Marsh before daylight. Frederick sat on the ground, knees up, head down, and I put the table over him. Then I covered it with some old blankets so that the "tablecloth" reached the ground and was lashed down to keep it from blowing and flapping in the northwest wind. And I arranged peepholes so he could watch the prairie chickens when—and if—they came.

By rights I should have been inside and under that card table, as I am considerably smaller and fold up far more comfortably. We planned it otherwise: my job was to flush the prairie chickens toward him. Perhaps if we had read the literature more carefully, we would have gathered that prairie cocks select a booming ground and only go to it if they want to.

I walked and waded the marshland; and every time I saw a likely spot for chickens to be, I detoured to flush any potential birds *toward* him. I persisted in this unprofitable undertaking with increasing, quiet frenzy for I knew that Frederick would stay put where he was, without moving, and never let me down. He'd stick it out under the card table until I flushed those birds toward him. The raw wind moaned above me as I ploshed through popple woods. I went in over my boot tops, and continued to plosh on as silently as I could, circling each grassy opening with what stealth I could muster.

Now and again I walked back to the edge of the vast opening—in part to make sure I wasn't lost—but it was also practical to know exactly where the card table was so I could steer any chickens that I might flush in the right direction.

After about two and a half hours of waiting, prairie chickens suddenly put in within sight of Frederick's card table of their own volition.

They stayed seven minutes.

The blind had worked! We were jubilant. Frederick said, "We'd better build another blind so we each have one." We constructed some wooden frames, covered them with old burlap bags, and allowed ourselves the luxury of an upside-down bucket to sit on. But the wind howled through the burlap and, worse still, so much light came in that whoever sat in the blind dared not move. Just opening a notebook and reaching for a pencil sometimes spooked the birds.

A trip to the town dump helped solve this problem. We found a soggy bedspread printed with pink roses, under a heap of tin cans; and we found a discarded circus poster blown against a battered car body. So much wealth gave great encouragement. We built two blinds and, as far as our material would last, we partially covered each: one with the pattern of roses shielding us from the sunny side and the other showing part of a lady riding part of a horse. Because we had our minds on the end product rather than on the ultimate effect, they were both upside down. Her legs in flesh-colored tights extended skyward and a little to the southeast; her toes barely touched the rump of a swiftly moving chestnut horse. If the neighbors started to talk we were unaware of it; our concern was with the prairie chickens. Both the lady and the roses were accepted by the birds, especially when the wind didn't cause the covering of our blinds to flap wildly and spook them.

The wind still roared into our blinds and we kept trying to tighten up loose edges of burlap, bedspread, and circus poster. At last Frederick said, "We need something better. We need a good, solid, dark blind. The worst thing about these is that they let in too much light."

"I'll take care of it."

Frederick looked at me in some surprise. "How?"

"I have an idea. I think I can get one in Wisconsin Rapids." Then I asked, "Do you want me to bring back anything else?"

"We need excelsior. It's high time we stuffed those birds." Every dead prairie chicken we found was autopsied and either made into a museum skin or otherwise stuffed.

That very afternoon I hooked up our eight-foot freight trailer and started off. There was a big store in town that sold furniture, refrigerators, and other large items; and such things were shipped in wooden packing boxes in those days. A piano crate would be too big, but a nice big refrigerator box would be perfect.

I drove into the alley behind the store and hesitated a moment; one could get into the store the back way, but it appeared to me that my chance of success might be improved by walking right in the front door like a customer. I combed my hair, added a little lipstick to my chapped lips, and turned the frayed cuffs of my jacket up inside the sleeves where they wouldn't show.

I walked right in the front door and sure enough a clerk came to welcome me. He had a pale face, thinning reddish hair and wore a cordial toothy smile. "Good afternoon."

"Good afternoon. Could you let me have a big box? I realize you must throw some away?"

He departed obligingly.

The store was big and dark and far from busy. It looked as though no one had shopped there for a week. Finally my friend the clerk returned still smiling and carrying a little box that could at most have contained a dozen blankets.

"Oh no," I exclaimed, extending my arms to give the impression of a huge box, "that won't do. You see my husband is going to be in it. He's big."

The clerk's pale face became, if anything, paler. His smile faded to a look of toothy terror and he backed away from me, feeling his way between the sofas and chairs in the gloom. He pulled away until he reached a small door and fumbled for the knob. Suddenly he was gone. Perhaps I imagined it, but I thought I heard him turn the key in the lock.

Kindness prompted me to go knock on that door and explain, but common sense won. I don't think that man ever wanted to see me again.

Somewhat dispirited I left and went down the street, into the alley, and back to the car. I glanced sadly at the empty trailer and then looked once more at the big back door of the store.

The door was ajar! I jumped up onto the loading platform and peered inside. There, recently pried open and empty except for some fine excelsior, was a sturdy big box. A huge man in overalls emerged from behind some machinery and said, "What da ya want?"

"I want that box, can I have it?"

"Yup." He offered to dump the excelsior, but I said I could use that too, so he just helped me load the box into the trailer.

"What da ya want the box *for?*"

"It's for watching birds."

"Yeah, and what's the excelsior for?"

"To put inside birds."

Suddenly he laughed with boisterous appreciation. He plainly cottoned to a girl with a quick tongue who liked to tell tall tales.

Rather anxiously I asked, "Could you tell the man in the front of the store what it's for?"

"Him? That fraidycat?" I was treated to a solemn wink, "You told *him* and he didn't believe you? I'll fix him!" he chuckled.

My burly friend headed for the front of the store, little suspecting that "fraidycat" was hiding back of a locked door—a door locked against a woman who was about to put her husband in a box. I had plenty to think about on the way home.

Frederick, bless him, admired the box and my neat haul of excelsior as well. "Did you have to pay for the box?" he asked.

"No, it was free. I got it for nothing."

"You sound a little subdued. Where'd you get the box?"

"In the furniture store. Nobody believed me there."

"Nobody believed you?"

"No, and the clerk thought I was going to put *you* in it."

Frederick looked utterly mystified. "I hope this box is not going to be exclusively for *your* use? I *will* be in it, won't I?"

"Yes, darling, but you see he thought you were going in piecemeal."

46

"What?"

"There's a man in that store who is very afraid of me."

Frederick can be wonderful. He simply studied my face for a moment or two and then spoke softly. "It's been a long day, hasn't it?"

He has a beautiful voice like dark chocolate.

Diseases, *not only shock* *but sack and sock*

Finally we built ourselves several good blinds covered with canvas. The chickens we had banded in winter wore aluminum bands on which remarkably small numbers had been stamped. Hunched in our new blinds, we tried to read the numbers of displaying chickens. Furthermore, we used binoculars. Spotting scopes were not yet in common use. Reading band numbers on cocks was not easy; as the hens spent most of their time low in the thickest vegetation, it was essentially impossible to read their numbers. We decided to settle for the cocks. Our hope was to read every cock's band on every booming

THE CHICKENS WORE ALUMINUM BANDS

ground to see where the birds we had caught in winter had gone to display in spring. The only way we could accomplish this was to spend very few mornings on each booming ground and then move the blind to another. To my chagrin, I had spent almost a week on one booming ground because one lone cock persisted in booming on a faraway knoll. I couldn't even tell whether or not he was banded—much less read his numbers!

On Easter morning a huge white bird flew right in front of my face, and I peeped cautiously out of the blind window. I thought it was a gull. Then I lifted the flap of another window and beheld that this monstrous bird wasn't a gull at all. It was a snowy owl—the first that I'd ever seen—and it was sitting on top of the very chicken I needed to check for bands.

Without a moment's hesitation, I pushed my way out the door flap of the blind and rushed to grab that chicken from her. The owl hopped only about three or four feet away, unwilling to relinquish

DECIPHERING NOTES
AT THE END OF
THE MORNING

her quarry. I seized the incapacitated cock, and the owl started to follow me back to the blind. Maybe I could catch the owl too!

Quickly I unlaced one of my tall boots and tied the chicken's legs together. Then I held the fluttering chicken out of the door slot. The owl bobbed its head and walked a few steps toward the blind. It moved faster, almost flying to reach this delectable meal again. I lay on the floor of the blind ready to grab its legs. Victory was within a few yards when this unusual activity attracted a flock of crows. They dive-bombed and harassed the owl until it gave up and took off in the pale rosy light of the sunrise. By then the prairie chicken had died of puncture wounds. It was unbanded; but anyway, I almost hand-grabbed the first snowy owl I ever saw and I did not toss the chicken carcass into an incinerator!

In 1940 it was neither bad form nor illegal to eat what unexpectedly came our way (out-of-season deer meat was the only exception). Nowadays if a biologist has no scientific use for a carcass, he must turn it over to a public institution "through channels," bury it, or burn it. I was very careful not to burn the carcass of the prairie chicken killed by the snowy owl. I roasted it in a hot oven for exactly twenty-five minutes. Joe Hickey, a fellow graduate student, was helping us out for a few days. Luncheon on Easter Sunday was the best meal any of us had had in some time.

I would like to add that the very idea of killing anything out of season for our own selfish use as food was inconceivable. We had too high a regard for our profession.

Having a prairie chicken in our hands during the booming season cemented our determination to color-mark the cocks on our booming grounds. We made bow nets, stapled them down carefully in the heart of what we believed to be individual territories, and ran a long string to the blind. It was hard to tell when the cock I was after was well centered in the bow net, but I gave a mighty pull when I figured he was in position and netted my bird. I put him into a sock and reset for another.

The next cock I tried for simply stamped along the edge of the bow net and never got inside the magic circle.

At the end of the morning's work I ran jubilantly toward Frederick shouting, "I caught! I caught!"

Frederick seemed a bit subdued. "I caught too, but my bird is dead."

I handed him the sock heavy with my bird, to raise his spirits. It was strangely inert: my bird was dead too.

We called it "sock disease" and decided that prairie cocks are more sensitive during the booming season and cannot be left lying around in socks as they can in winter.

R. K. Meyer, the endocrinologist, autopsied those birds for us and could come up with only one tentative conclusion: hypoglycemia—shock disease.

He gave us each a vial of sugar solution and a syringe. "Next time just inject warm sugar solution quickly, and maybe the bird will come out of it all right."

For some years thereafter we each wore a vial of sugar solution next to our skin to keep the solution warm, and we each carried a syringe. There never was a next time. We encountered this unhappy phenomenon just once. After the double accident, we processed and released booming-ground birds far more quickly than winter birds. Now that I look back on it, it seems that our early diagnosis of sock disease was correct.

Sack disease is not the same. We soon learned that in winter if we had a good catch, we'd better not put more than five birds into one burlap bag, lest those on the bottom smother.

Imping

Early in the spring the prairie cocks rush about on the booming grounds and fight. Usually the fights draw no blood. Prairie cocks have no spurs, but they fight each other with their feet and wings— and they bite. Feathers are strewn all over the booming ground and sometimes the fights are prolonged and violent. The lack of an umpire in wildlife fights makes them far more exciting to watch than TV. The fights are real and not for money.

Frederick and I tried to figure out why cocks never killed each other outright. The whole performance of sixteen or so cocks tearing around a booming ground, fighting, blowing up their huge orange air sacs, and booming lacked pattern. This behavior started each year in late February or in March . . . long before any hens appeared on the booming grounds. It looked like merry mayhem without a purpose. The terms "territory," and "appeasement behavior," were not yet common in the ornithological literature of the 1930s and early 1940s.

We were baffled and nobody needed to tell us what must be done next: we must individually color-mark as many cocks as possible on at least two booming grounds. Fearing shock, or some other related "disease," we had all our materials in readiness before we started to net prairie cocks—one after another—on the booming grounds. If we could manage it, every cock was going to wear brightly colored tail feathers or neck tufts.

We saved feathers from dead bluejays and cardinals, pulled feathers from the speculums of duck wings to put in the neck tufts of living cock prairie chickens; and we dyed quantities of white feathers red, green, blue, and yellow to imp their tails.

The word "imp" comes from the Latin word *imponere,* to place within. Falconers were not only the first ethologists, but they were also the first group of people that really understood the care of individual birds. As an example, when a flight feather broke, they mended it by imping a new one.

52

We adapted the falconers' technique, but with something very different in mind! Instead of adding part of a matching feather we strove for conspicuous mismatches.

Each time we succeeded in catching a cock, we cut off a feather quite close to the skin, but so the hollow shaft of the feather protruded. Then we selected some brightly colored feather that would fit neatly into the hollow shaft. Having made sure that the fit was good, we plunged the base of the colored feather into Duco household cement and then fitted it into the cut shaft on the bird itself. The cement dried in about two minutes and—with luck—the cock would wear the brightly colored feather for months—until the next molt. Imping the tip of a feather worked better on the pinnae—the long, earlike tufts of feathers on each side of the neck.

At last all the cocks on the booming ground didn't look alike to us. There is something very frustrating about having a whole bunch of birds rushing about in front of you day after day without knowing what they are doing or who they are. But even before we had trapped many, we came to realize that certain places were "pet spots" of certain cocks, and that our best chance of catching a given individual was in his pet spot.

53

The recognition of "pet spots" would seem to have established that prairie chicken cocks are territorial on their booming grounds: not at all! The unravelling of the mystery was like a detective story.

In the first place, "pink tuft right" had two pet spots. Sometimes he boomed on one and then he flew across the booming ground and displayed on the other.

In the second place, *visiting* cocks sometimes appeared. These tended to scoot around the booming ground with their bodies held low and their pinnae lowered, but sometimes they "gained courage" and boomed, and a very few even set up a territory!

Most confusing of all was the electric change that came over a booming ground when hens appeared. One hen could drive sixteen cocks to distraction. I mean distraction in the exact sense of the word: the cocks were distracted from their territories. Even one hen walking the booming ground precipitates a type of frenzy. She doesn't have to do anything; she may just pick at a few willow buds and scratch imaginary lice from time to time, seemingly unaware of all the cocks displaying around her.

At last we saw that the influence of one or more hens pulls the territories of the cocks out of shape like a pencil drawn through an outspread hair net. The nearer the hen, the greater the distraction, and the more the cocks "forget" their territories.

We needed to fit one more piece into the puzzle before we could be certain that prairie cocks were territorial, and within two years the missing piece was found: prairie chickens can distinguish each other's sex by behavior only! This is very strange because any beginner can learn that the neck tufts of the cock are about three inches long and those of the hen are far shorter—only about one inch. Any cock that behaves like a hen and keeps his neck tufts down is "treated like a lady." Any hen that raises her long slender neck with its short pinnae has declared her true sex—female.

We published our findings on territorialism in a gallinaceous species in 1949. That same year David Lack published on territories of British black grouse, a species with a similar display. He cannot have had the fun that we had, because black cocks are big and mostly black and the hens are far smaller and brown.

They can tell each other's sex at a glance.

DARK NEAR EYES ·
DARK QUAD
DEEP NECKLACE

WHITE BOTH SIDES OF EYES
FAINT QUAD
PEARL NECKLACE

DARK NEAR EYES
DEEP SMOKEY QUAD
GRASSY STREAKED NECKLACE

WHITE BEFORE EYES
FAINT LINE QUAD
NECKLACE HAS RIGHT BLOB

How to tell chickens by their faces

It has always amazed me that grade school teachers can memorize the names of twenty to thirty children in one morning, and correctly associate the right name with the right child. This is phenomenal.

I've queried quite a few teachers about this. They are pleased at my sincere admiration of their feat, and not infrequently they ask, "Why do you want to know?"

"Well, I study birds and I'd like to learn your technique."

Not one could teach me his technique, so I developed one of my own and now grade school teachers find me phenomenal: I can tell individual prairie chickens apart!

The trick is to give each bird a *name*. A cock who favors his left foot and hobbles about becomes "Lame left." It took Frederick to point out that only if the leg has sustained a permanent injury will he always be "Lame left." After all, he might get well!

The most reliable way of telling prairie chickens apart is by their faces. The bird-book names for the parts of a bird's head were cumbersome and didn't fit our need for quick descriptions just to name and recognize individuals. There is an area near the quadrate bone, close to the angle of the jaw, that ranges from solid black, to smoky, to freckled, to pale, to no markings at all. The areas just before and just back of the eyes may be white, mottled, or dark. The necklace at the base of the neck varies enormously; it may be deep, narrow, pale, or even asymmetrical.

55

I have mentioned four parts that can be described, and once we got the hang of it, it was just as easy as memorizing red hair—freckles—tall—ears stick out.

Hens tend to remain sleek, are not seen repeatedly, and are far harder to memorize than cocks.

By the time the booming season is at its peak and the hens are finally appearing on the booming grounds, most of the cocks are so battle scarred that we can recognize them by knocked out tail feathers, broken primaries, and puncture wounds on their air sacs.

Feathers are eventually replaced, wounds heal, and we know that the names we give these cocks will not all carry through until next spring. It takes but a moment to sketch the puncture wounds on the left or right air sac of a cock, but again it was Frederick who sounded a warning note.

"That cock, dark quad, white back of eye, and checkered necklace, is right in front of my blind. I sketched the puncture wounds on his left air sac."

I nodded enthusiastically, having just found puncture wounds useful.

"Here are my sketches at twenty-minute intervals," he muttered angrily. "Those puncture wounds were ticks—just ticks—walking across the air sac."

Aunt Ruby's box

It always gave us delight to drive down our long driveway flanked by tall pines. Not until we reached the walnut grove could we see our beautifully proportioned house and marvel that Walter Ware, a pioneer, had fitted the low, simple lines of New England farmhouses into the Wisconsin landscape.

We never locked our doors and we never worried about having anybody steal anything. . . .

Late one afternoon we drove home through the pines, but when we got to the walnut grove, I gasped, "Somebody's stolen the windows!"

Frederick pressed his foot on the gas pedal, and as we roared nearer he sounded incredulous. "The windows are still there; they just took the glass!"

We rushed into the house so we could see how much damage had been done. No breeze blew into the rooms; the windows were still there. Somebody had *washed* the glass in all the windows of the whole house. Instead of the dead fisheye look that we'd become accustomed to, the panes were so clean that it appeared they were absent; when the light struck them just right they sparkled.

Two monogrammed bath towels from my trousseau, with dirt ground into them beyond recovery, were stuffed into an old pot. There was a small, neat note on the kitchen table. The Mannegolds— German-American aristocracy—had driven up from Milwaukee to see us. They had waited and had decided to do something useful while waiting.

I wrote Frederick's Aunt Ruby, wife of the criminal lawyer Clarence Darrow, about the day we thought the windows had been stolen, and how we could buy milk for five cents a quart if we supplied the bottle tops (which I cut out of cardboard with my manicure scissors), and various details of our rural housekeeping. It was fun to write to her: she was the only member of the family who didn't consider me "plucky"; she didn't criticize my housekeeping, and she sent extraordinary Christmas boxes.

Not long after my letter, Aunt Ruby's box arrived; we opened it eagerly. Neither of us had had enough to eat on a regular basis for several years. I had even come down with a mild case of beriberi and food was never far from our thoughts.

Each item in Aunt Ruby's box was labeled, and most labels contained a message or admonition. I wish I'd saved some of her bizarre little notes. Some were scrawled in purple ink, and others had been dashed off on one of the first "silent portable typewriters." The individually wrapped packages were packed—or shall I say "floated"—with masses of ribbon-cut waxed paper that I had normally associated with Easter eggs.

"When your Uncle Clarence and I were in Hawaii, we became very fond of these little fish. You will note that they are preserved in wine. Do *NOT*!!! serve them with wine. Buy some *unsalted* crackers and serve them with very fine brandy, and *do* save them for special occasions."

The same box contained a large bottle labeled "Applejack"— which turned out to be the very fine brandy.

"Have been saving milk bottle tops for Fran. Enclosed are 56. They can be washed several times."

"The maid tells me that the hotel is throwing away a quantity of towels and sheets. Your Uncle Clarence and I find nothing wrong with them. After sheets tear, they can be made into pillowcases, and old towels can be cut up for washrags.''

It is now forty years later and we still have a few items of linen labeled *St. George Hotel.*

''A newspaper man—delightful, and a great admirer of Clarence—sent us some Russian caviar. Norman Thomas and Lillian Gish thought it perfectly delicious.''

The package contained *eighteen* large tins of imported caviar.

''Do eat this little tin of tongue, smoked in wine, *all by yourselves*!!!!!''

''These little packages of cheeses come from a Norwegian acquaintance. Are you aware that your Uncle Burt believes that part of the Hamerstrom family came from Norway?'' We ripped open one package of cheese, a little round box—and guzzled Gruyère—perfectly aged Gruyère. Then we opened a tin of caviar and I sliced some homemade bread. The first bite was delicious, but have you ever tried eating caviar without butter or margarine? We could afford neither.

Matter-of-factly I said, ''Let's save the caviar for tonight's meat.'' I pulled frost-bitten leaves off an old cabbage head and cooked up the whitened inside leaves. Then I sorted out the food from Aunt Ruby's box and put it on the kitchen table. That sparkling display of luxuries must have cost at least $60—more than we earned in a month—and there was no way we could convert it to cash to buy potatoes.

After supper I picked up the milk bottle tops, sheets, shirts, and miscellany to put them away. An old hat, passed down from Aunt Ruby, was remarkably heavy. It was rolled around a large tin of pickled lamb's tongues. Then I took all the crinkly green paper out of the box to make sure that nothing had been missed.

There was one more item: a package of three bars of Pear's soap with a note wrapped around it, ''Remember to visit Arthur Krock. He can help you in many ways. Fran can go too. Just tell him who you are.'' Aunt Ruby didn't need to spell it out: Frederick was to tell Mr. Krock—or whoever else was recommended to us—that he was Clarence Darrow's nephew. We never went to see any of these people; none of them were biologists.

Pear's is still my favorite soap.

Plenty of sunlight

We knew we were good at nest finding. When we had worked under Paul Errington in Iowa, we had proven it. We had found 503 pheasant nests. Now we tried the same techniques—searching methodically in likely looking terrain—and failed to turn up a single prairie chicken nest. Farmers found them while haying, foresters found them while tree-planting, but we couldn't find a single nest. We decided to change our tactics and mark down where the hens went after a successful copulation. Maybe they went straight to the vicinity of the nest site! But we didn't give up our old pheasant approach. We still walked the Leola Marsh looking for nests. Dragging a rope between us and the occasional use of a borrowed pointing dog were no more successful. We *never* found a nest.

The farmers, however, watched these goings-on with a great deal of tolerance. Sometimes they asked what we were doing, but more often they asked why we didn't have any children. We explained that in 1935 we had decided that the world, *including* the United States, was overpopulated and that we had decided to have only two children and to have them late in life. Our primitive contraceptives worked for nine years and then we deliberately discontinued using them. (One was a mixture of cocoa butter, quinine, and something else, brewed on the kitchen stove in tin cigarette boxes.)

One evening I made a dramatic announcement. "Darling, I think we are going to have a baby. My stomach feels all funny and bloated."

Frederick didn't even look up from the book he was reading. He just said, "So does mine."

I dismissed the whole idea, but I made a mark on the calendar.

Thirty-five days later I knew. After an especially hard, hot day in the field, I lay down on the blue sofa and announced, "We *are* going to have a baby!" I lay on the sofa waiting. The deep wisdom of my man still fascinates me. He didn't say a thing and didn't look up from his book.

I waited for him to come to fan me with a magazine, or to hold my hand and to murmur, "Are you all right?"

He did nothing of the sort. As far as I could tell he kept right on reading his damned book.

After what seemed about twenty minutes he remarked, "It's your turn to get the water."

We pumped the water into big, heavy milk cans and lugged them into the house. Ladies in a delicate condition were not even supposed to hang up a picture!

Quivering with outrage and indignation, I lay on the sofa and glared. At last I got up and pumped all that water and carried it into the house. It was a turning point in our lives. I stayed on the sofa a long time before I got up and did it, but it was one of the best things that ever happened to me.

Motherhood was not going to smash a research team which has now lasted forty-eight years.

Frederick's concern for me was not only psychological but also practical. He got Eddie Gordon, our family doctor, to refer me to the very best obstetrician in Madison. As it happened, Dr. M. was a "society-type doctor," unaccustomed to wildlife biologists.

The doctor examined me and said, "You are three months pregnant. Why didn't you come sooner?"

I didn't like to explain that when my stomach had felt all funny and bloated, Frederick and I had both attributed these symptoms to indigestion. I just hung my head.

Then I did some quick mathematics. "That means the baby will be born about *October*!"

October was right in the hunting season! Could unkind fate incapacitate me during the time of year we both most looked forward to? It didn't, but Dr. M. and I had no idea that my hunting season was safe and that I was about to be delivered of a ten-month baby— not a nine month's pregnancy, but *ten*.

Dr. M. said, "You'd better give up tennis."

Tennis flashed across my mind. My governess had taught me lawn tennis with the graceful underhand serve; then at Milton Academy I was taught the overhand serve; and then a new tennis instructor had come, the very year the Japanese were winning matches by shifting racquets from hand to hand. His first ambidextrous pupil sent him into transports, and he gave me a lot of lessons my parents never paid for!

Tennis was part of the world I'd left behind. I said only, "All right."

"But you may continue to play golf." Golf! That dull game

that I'd been forced to play to be polite and to make up a foursome to oblige my father's old cronies!

Again I just said, "All right."

Dr. M. had not forbidden me to hunt ducks and prairie chickens; he had not forbidden me to climb trees to band hawks. I left well enough alone, even when he put me on a strict diet.

He appeared somewhat puzzled that I had not put up any arguments. He needed some sort of rebuttal to size up his patient. I can see his point. I think he—quite rightly—had the uneasy feeling that I was not trustworthy. He was right; if he had ordered me not to hunt, I would have disobeyed and said nothing.

He countered with an absolute rule: "I insist that you get plenty of sunlight." To tennis and golf I had not registered in the normal manner of his usual patients. "Do you *promise* me that you will get plenty of sunlight?"

"Yes."

This promise didn't give him much grief until I came in for a late summer checkup. I had spent many hours looking for prairie chicken nests and gathering vast quantities of blueberries, blackberries, and some raspberries. The country was wilder then and far more thinly populated. It was my custom to hang my dress from the handle of my berry basket so that I could slip it on quickly if I spotted somebody in the distance.

Dr. M. started with questions.

"Morning sickness?"

"No."

"Backache?"

"No."

"Discomfort?"

"I'm hungry all the time. If I were a cow, I'd be getting all I wanted to eat."

"A *cow*?" Dr. M. laid down his pen. "What's a cow got to do with it?"

I should have explained that Frederick and I had minored in veterinary medicine. Instead I spoke with simple authority. "Pregnant animals shouldn't be starved."

"You're not starved."

"I am. Ask Dr. Gordon."

Reluctantly Dr. M. called him in for consultation, and Eddie asked, "How much walking are you doing, Fran?"

"Ten to fifteen miles a day I suppose—maybe more." I handed Eddie my diet: four ounces of meat, one slice of toast, lettuce, tomatoes, and so forth. Eddie, bless him, suggested that I be taken off the diet entirely. He winked, shook hands with Frederick, and left.

Dr. M. hadn't needed to ask me whether or not I was getting plenty of sunlight. My face and neck and arms were so deeply tanned that my eyeballs showed strangely white. A nurse steered me into a little side room, told me to undress, slip into a stiff white garment, and lie on the table. Then she covered me with a sheet and departed. In a moment or two Dr. M. started his examination. There seemed to be something wrong with his breathing. He raised the sheet and the garment higher and higher. When he came to the white semicircles under my breasts he sputtered, ''How do you feel?''

''Fine.''

He pulled down the garment, replaced the sheet, and departed in haste.

Frederick, having had a look at the doctor's face, pushed his way past the nurse and asked, ''Are you all right?''

''Yes. I don't know what's gotten into him.''

I was getting a bit scared myself, and when Dr. M. arrived with another doctor, I studied the two worried faces and my alarm grew.

Then, suddenly, I knew exactly what was wrong: neither of these dear gentlemen had ever examined a white female patient who had spent essentially all summer out in the sun without clothes!

I started quivering and choking, which must have added to their alarm, but I was only trying to suppress my laughter. Then I tried to sit up to explain and was pushed firmly back down. It was very hard on all three of us. They must have thought that I had Addison's disease, and here I was trying to explain that I hung my dress on the handle of a basket. Perhaps they thought my mind was slipping too.

Finally I had to overcome my reticence and spell it out for them. ''You said I was to get plenty of sunlight. I did. I went *naked!*''

Life will never be the same again school of thought

Mrs. Leopold and her circle of friends very kindly invited me to attend meetings of The Reading Club—known irreverently by the younger generation as The Eating Club. I liked to go to their meetings and savored both the learning and the little cakes that were served afterwards.

As soon as The Reading Club discovered that I was expecting a baby, I was bombarded with advice, admonitions, and even commands:

You will have to give up your wild ways and tend to your baby.

You can no longer live up north in that unheated house.

You and Frederick must move to Madison; he can do the field work on weekends. You will find that a baby is a big responsibility and will take just about all your time.

All these delightful ladies had children. "*Unutterably depressing*" was my reaction to their comments.

I enumerated what I had learned from The Reading Club to Frederick on our way home to our beloved prairie chicken country.

He stopped me when I repeated, "You can no longer live up north. . . ."

"How about the Eskimos?"

Suddenly we were both laughing uproariously. We gave The Reading Club still another name: we called it *The Life Will Never Be the Same Again School of Thought*. Having given them a new name, we could reexamine their values. We were free.

In spring I had teetered on Frederick's sunburned shoulders for a "leg up" to band young red-tailed hawks. In summer I had tromped the marshes and meadows to look for prairie chicken nests and to gather winter stores of wild foods. And then when the leaves of the popples turned gold and the hunting season opened, we spent much of our time hunting.

It was always a disappointment to me that Frederick insisted that essentially every bird we killed had to be made into a museum specimen. To retain the best flavor of the rich, dark meat, prairie chickens, shot in the Lake States, are best roasted for a short time in a hot oven and *with the skin on*.

We had no idea how to tell which chickens had hatched the preceding spring and which were older. Aldo Leopold always came up to hunt chickens with us, and our hunting pattern did not change. We started early in the morning, flushed a flock from a grainfield, and followed it. Following a flock of prairie chickens is rather like following a big game animal: one learns its habits largely by reading sign. Shotgun in hand, we learned a great deal about their autumn habits.

FREDERICK IMITATES
THE PROFESSOR'S STANCE

At noon we cooked lunch, building a small fire and often just roasting meat over oak coals with an apple or two as a side dish. Then, if the day was pleasant, we basked on a sandbank and talked over various matters. Leopold unobtrusively led the discussion. "Why do prairie chickens undergo a ten-year cycle? Why does the population *crash* about every ten years and then come up again?

65

"We've got to understand the pulse of this phenomenon. Do they sometimes breed at an accelerated rate? Is the rate the same at low densities? Read Charles Elton. We must learn to count those chickens and find a way to distinguish between the young birds and the older ones. . . ."

Then we stamped out the ashes of our cook fire and hunted until dusk. We came back to our house in the pines. We drank whiskey out of tin cups and I cooked supper. The fire popped and crackled and then died down. We talked. Aldo reiterated. "Count those chickens. Get counts of the winter flocks."

"But we counted and trapped a winter flock of thirty and kept trapping and caught thirty more," I interjected.

Frederick simply said, "Aldo, it appears to me that winter is the worst possible time to count chickens. If we want to learn what is happening here, we must count in spring."

"Well, they've got to be counted."

Aldo in the handsome tweed hunting garb he always wore, leaned across my kitchen table to add, "And remember production. Can you distinguish between birds of the year and old birds yet?"

With Aldo's admonition in mind I went out to get specimens to see if I could find a way to tell the young birds from the old. I was collecting, which is not as much fun as hunting—the ulterior motive subtly subverts hunting to "work." At any rate I spotted a prairie chicken sitting on top of a haystack in a farmyard. I sneaked up on it, never suspecting that I was being watched. Gun in hand I crawled on all fours through a muddy puddle not unvisited by cows, between the house and the barn.

When I got close enough I let fly with my shotgun, a Parker 20-gauge; and my prize slid slowly down the haystack and landed on its back.

The farmer roared from his doorway. At first I didn't quite catch what he was yelling. He shouted, "Nice shot!" Then he added, "Come in and have a cup of coffee."

Chicken in hand, my gun at rest in the crook of my arm, I walked toward the doorstep.

"Didn't know it was a lady!"

I felt it my duty to explain the difference between collecting and hunting and I wanted to explain that I would never shoot any bird in such an unsporting manner except for collecting, but I was "outnumbered" by the joyous enthusiasm of one farmer. ". . . belly-crawled all the way from the gate. That chicken didn't have a *chance*." Hunting was different in those days.

It was at about this time that I remembered how Harry Pry, an old Scottish gamekeeper, had taught me the way to kill upland game birds so they would pluck easily. "Bite them in the head, right back of both ears, and it relaxes their feathers so they just fall off."

We didn't want the feathers to fall off the chickens, because we wanted to make museum skins of them. But it gave such a quick easy death that I bit a few heads and discovered something very interesting: birds of the year "bit easily" and older birds had tough, entirely resistant skulls. Long before other techniques were worked out, we had found a way to age prairie chickens.

We soon set up the Hamerstrom free plucking service: "for *nothing* we will pluck your prairie chickens and get them oven-ready." We drove around the marsh and wherever we found hunters who had been successful, we made our sales pitch. We didn't study the hunters carefully; we just tried to make sure that we could get our hands on their birds. The hunters, I later learned, studied us with some amazement. They watched us sort out the chickens by sex according to feather pattern; and then they watched me pluck each bird, eviscerate it, look at the gonads, and hand Frederick the crop and gizzard. Of course we were not plucking those birds for *nothing*: we wanted information on age, food habits, parasites, and such things. Frederick told the hunters what we were doing and why—in part to keep them entertained while they waited for me to finish plucking.

After the material we wanted was safely in labeled paper bags, there came a moment when I had to interrupt, "You don't mind if I bite their heads do you?"

I don't believe a single hunter answered me with a clear-cut, "Yes, go right ahead." Many gave the impression that they had not correctly heard what I had said! Nobody said, "No," so whatever sounds they made after I posed the question, I went right ahead and bit heads. The birds lay in a row on the ground and Frederick had the paper bags ready in the same order. I glanced quickly at each bird to make sure my bite would come just back of the ears and called out my results, "Bit easy . . . bit easy . . . hard . . . shot-up (can't use that one) . . . bit easy . . . bit easy, no, let me get this one again. Darling, it bit easy, but it seems harder than most of the young birds. Maybe it hatched earlier?" Frederick recorded the information on each bag. Later we found more scientific-looking ways of determining age.

Later, in fact many years later, old prairie chicken hunters still would come up to me, waggling a finger gleefully in my face, "I know you. You're the one that bit them heads!"

Dental floss

We hunted hard and checked other hunters' birds day after day. In the evenings we worked the bars in a nearby town. Frederick took those on one side of the street and I took the other. Successful hunters, as well as the unsuccessful, sat on barstools and told stories in the evenings. To get our hands on more specimens, we listened to separate the former from the latter and then offered the Hamerstrom free plucking service. It was a lot less work for a hunter to get up and open the trunk of his car and let us get his birds oven-ready than to take them home and have to do the job himself. Some hunters just handed me their car keys and said, "Go ahead."

Frederick detested working the bars. There is something about his kindly face and manner that attracts drunks like flies to a jampot. They put their arms around his shoulders, some even weep; and they tell him the sad story of their lives. Not letting go of his shoulders, they weave to and fro, and my delightful husband has never found a way of extricating himself.

Never in all my life have I encountered anyone with such a strong sense of duty as Frederick. No matter how unpleasant, distasteful, or boring an undertaking may be, his conscience forces him to finish it or do it again if the *work* requires that it be done. I'm better at visiting sick aunts and things like that. And I'm better at visiting bars.

I found the bars fun. Innumerable beery gents and some perfectly sober ones offered me drinks and sometimes, when all the birds had been bitten, robbed of their crops and gizzards, and returned neatly to the cars, I accepted a drink—not beer but a glass of port—and joined in the hunting yarns myself.

Each evening, after we had worked the bars, we looked for each other. The main street of Hancock was only a little over a block long, so this was not much of a problem. If Frederick found me first, he was apt to find me listening to some old hunter with rapt attention, "Got three in one shot; two fell into the willows, and I just wung the other. Spot," the hunter stroked the undistinguished head of a large mongrel at his feet, "this here's Spot. He's got dog sense; he went for the wung one first!"

"The wung one?"

"Yeah, just shot in the wing. I wung it."

The hunter looked around the room appreciatively and spotted Frederick.

"This must be your hubby! Come and have a drink. Your wife has been telling us the most interestin' stories."

Much as I wanted to stay, I knew it was impossible. Frederick had given me a look: it was time to go home. In fact it was time to get out right quick because a big farmer, deep in his cups, was already weaving his way directly toward my "hubby" to tell him all his teary troubles.

"Whoops!" I shouted. "We've got to get back and feed." I ran for the door, and Frederick, trying to give thanks for the proffered drink, was forced to cut them short in order to keep up with me.

We drove home in very different moods. After a while Frederick asked, "What are we going to feed?"

"Ourselves, I suppose." Frederick looked puzzled. "People will always let you go if you say, 'I gotta feed.' I was just trying to help you get out of there. You didn't want to *stay*, did you?"

"Good God no!"

The baby had been expected the last week in September, and October was already upon us. With some justice I might have pleaded my delicate condition, but such a softy approach never even entered my mind.

Frederick saw to it that the car always had plenty of gas each evening in case I should give a night alarm. After all, the doctor was 100 miles away. We continued with our normal and rather strenuous lives.

One day, just as a long string of geese passed over the marsh, I felt a little pain in my stomach and looked at my watch to note the time. Labor pains were supposed to start at twenty-minute intervals. The geese flew northwest and way out of sight. Then two mallards dropped into a ditch only about a half a mile away. When I got to the spot I'd marked down along the ditch bank, one flushed wild; I dropped the other right in the water: a fine greenhead to add to our meager larder.

My tennis shoes had come untied retrieving the duck, so I stopped at the top of the ditch bank to retie the laces. It was awkward to reach down to my foot. To my surprise Frederick, who was some distance away, drove the car right across a meadow and straight to where I was. "Are you all right?" he asked anxiously.

"Yes." I held up my dripping duck.

"You were in such an odd position. I thought the baby was coming. Let's settle on a signal," he continued, "When you think it's time to head for Madison, fire *three* equally spaced shots."

We agreed on this. Not until the rabbit season opened did he hear three equally spaced shots, and that time it was just rabbit hunters.

Frederick started carrying sterile dental floss in his pocket fearing he might have to deliver the baby and tie off its umbilical cord all by himself. After all it had been due in September. October had passed, and it was now *November!*

On November 8 we hunted ducks all day, then I helped carry in firewood for the winter and cooked supper. It was during supper that I had my first inkling that something might be about to happen. Unobtrusively, I put the kitchen clock where I could see it easily and marked down times on a piece of scratch paper. About forty minutes later I exclaimed, "We go!"

We started getting into city clothes. Having waded in peat most of the day—in jeans because I had no way of fastening my hip boots to a belt—I considered taking a bath and then decided against it because it took so long to heat up the bath water. I put on a skirt and pulled on some heavy, "service-weight" stockings.

About two and a half hours later I was sitting on the edge of a hospital bed begging a nurse to let me take a bath.

"No, Mrs. Hamerstrom. I hardly think that will be necessary."

I pulled down one stocking and the nurse disappeared with dispatch. She returned a moment later with a nurse wearing a different sort of cap—who took one look at my legs and said, "Mrs. Hamerstrom, if you feel up to it you may have a shower immediately."

Alan's birth certificate states under "duration of pregnancy": 10 months. It wasn't until Elva was born two years later that I realized that normal babies can look like embryo witches with red, puckered, disorganized faces, long fingernails, and unearthly black hair on their heads.

Alan looked like a cover photo on the *Ladies' Home Journal* with well-formed features and creamy, attractive skin. First, I took off his diaper to ascertain his sex for myself. Then I kissed the top of his head and started licking him. It was good. When Elva arrived, I was robbed of one of the joys of motherhood. Elva's skin tasted of some sort of medicinal soap.

It is a great pity that our research at the time our children were babies was on birds, rather than on mammals. I learned a few interesting things about mammals, but I wasn't really tuned in. I did have an opportunity to notice something about suckling rhythm, in spring when we were planting a long row of white pines to celebrate Alan's birth. One day when Frederick and I were slit-planting, I let my shovel slip from my hand and just walked back to the house without offering any explanation whatsoever. It was simply time to nurse my baby, and the signal from my body had been just as accurate and strong as if an alarm clock had gone off in my pocket.

When Elva was born, I was in the hospital exactly three days. She was wheeled into my room in some sort of a baby buggy with a squeaking wheel. I paid no attention to the squeaking wheel at the time and simply chafed because hospitals separated mother and baby except for the brief periods of nursing.

At the end of three days I returned home. Alan had a little toy cart that he liked to pull along the floor. A wheel of the cart squeaked and that squeak could set my milk to flowing—or if Elva heard it first, it set her to crying. Sometimes I think "civilization" is a bit nutty.

FRAN AND ELVA

71

Do you want to go to Africa?

Our house in the pines was not a bad place to bring up a baby. We could bank the fire in the wood stove so it would last all night. Country houses have cold floors and—as heat rises—any heated room is warmer up near the ceiling. We hung a thermometer on the edge of the baby basket, and raised or lowered the basket; so the baby, at least, would enjoy the right temperature most of the time.

There were other problems. Frederick had already put off getting his Ph.D. for a year so we could continue, with our stipend of $50 a month, to work on prairie chickens, but both of us knew that we couldn't live forever on this salary—cutting popple poles to make trap frames, making our own netting out of string, and going to burned-down houses to look for old nails to straighten, to hammer prairie chicken traps together. Now that there were three of us, it was time to get a "pay job". . . and there were no prairie chicken jobs available.

Most especially, there was no job that could keep us working on the chicken population we had worked on so long, so in the spring of 1941 Frederick accepted a secure position as curator of the Edwin S. George Reserve, a division of the Museum of Zoology of the University of Michigan . . . with freedom to work on anything we wanted to. Frederick stipulated that he wanted to take his vacation in the hunting season, and Mr. Gaige, director of the museum—somewhat puzzled—acquiesced. We had a surprise in store: not only were there to be vacations, but *expeditions* as well. In March, Mr. Gaige proposed to Frederick that he might want to go on an expedition for a month or so.

Frederick's answer was prompt and enthusiastic. "Oh, *yes*, could we go in April? That would be just right; we need to continue our count of the prairie chickens on the Leola Marsh in Wisconsin." We went, and our baby spent much of his time in upside-down prairie chicken traps instead of a playpen, or in the back of the car, which we had fixed up for him.

Just a year later Mr. Gaige again raised the question of going on an expedition, but this time he made his intention quite clear, "Would you like to go to South America? Or perhaps Africa?"

Frederick admitted that we would love to go to Africa, but stated that it was of the utmost urgency to return to the Leola Marsh to count chickens. Mr. Gaige agreed, but it was plain that South America—or Timbuktu—would have pleased him more.

By the third spring, World War II had started. Africa was out of the question. Mr. Gaige told us where to apply for a permit to get gasoline to go on a "scientific expedition" to Wisconsin.

Alan, our inquisitive two-year-old, had outgrown playpens. Our neighbors, "Uncle Warren" and "Aunt Ethel," would keep him while we were away. That settled, we went to the courthouse to apply for the permit. The long flight of courthouse steps had me puffing and I was wearing Frederick's old plaid shirt—my "maternity smock."

The man giving out permits was neither friendly nor unfriendly.

"Scientific expedition?"

"Yes."

He wrote this down. "To Wisconsin?"

"Yes."

Again the pencil filled in a blank on the form.

"Personnel and equipment: how many of you will be going?"

Frederick and I answered simultaneously.

Frederick said, "Two," but I said, "Three." I gave Frederick a sharp kick in the shin and repeated, *"Three."*

"Equipment?"

"Yes, traps and blinds."

He shoved the paper toward Frederick and said, "Sign this."

Frederick signed it unhappily. As soon as we were out of earshot, he demanded, "What made you say *three?* You know Alan will be staying with Aunt Ethel."

"I know, but there's a better chance of getting gas with three going."

Frederick spoke in anger, "What got into you? There'll be *two.* Just you and me."

We stood on the courthouse steps and argued. "I'm going back to change it to two. I won't sign my name to a lie."

"But, darling, it won't be a lie. Did you forget that we'll have the next baby before we leave!"

Lumbago

The war years and to a large degree the five years in southern Michigan separated us from our chickens. Try as we might, we couldn't forget that in central Wisconsin lay a wilder, more untamed country and that we wanted to work on prairie chickens more than anything else in the world.

In 1949 we pulled up stakes and left a modern rent-free house and a secure job. I have always been impressed that Frederick, with two small children to support, had the courage to quit when he felt he should.

We wanted to work together, but most administrators were afraid to hire a female biologist. After weeks of job hunting a telegram came. The Wisconsin Conservation Department wanted a prairie chicken biologist and would hire *me* too! So we found and fixed up another abandoned farmhouse—a big house with a ballroom that had never been finished because the boys had to go away to fight in the Civil War!

All this was extraordinary luck. Our next stroke of luck was, I'm sorry to say, the misfortune of a neighbor.

The lumbago of John Rozner may have altered our whole lives. John lived in the far north end of our study area some twenty miles from our house. Little did we dream that the miserable pain in his lower back in the autumn would cause us to make a record catch of prairie chickens.

Pain caused him to stay indoors as much as possible, and he just couldn't manage to harvest his corn. The shocks stood in the field ready to harvest, and then the snows came—the deep, deep snows came and prairie chickens congregated. They were hungry and consumed the corn from the outsides of the shocks until there was practically nothing left for them to eat.

The vast number of hungry prairie chickens trying to eke out an existence in the Rozner corn made us realize that we were dealing

74

with a pack! Packing is a phenomenon that the early settlers described in various imaginative ways, and perhaps my description is imaginative too. It seems to be the result of a "snowballing" effect: young chickens stay near their mothers until about September, then these family units merge and are joined by miscellaneous cocks to make flocks of thirty or so, which hang together. Sometimes, but not every winter, the flocks merge and form *packs*. Packs may consist of two or three hundred birds. When flushed from corn stubble, they zoom out of the field like bees from a hive; they circle and take off in a great body heading away over the popple woods, the marshes, and the farmlands.

The Rozner pack was plainly a most unusual opportunity. Four of us undertook to trap it: Frederick and I and Os and Mary Mattson. We moved traps by trailer—about eight at a time.

George Socha

Finally, we had hauled forty-eight traps from stations miles away and made our biggest set to date. It was perfect timing—food supply almost exhausted and birds still coming in to feed. Actually, I have a hunch that the Rozner station was a turning point in our skill as trappers and in our efficiency as biologists. I shudder to think how often we had just placed a trap or two wherever we saw chicken tracks. The morning catch on March 13, 1950, was good, but the afternoon catch shortly before sundown was almost more than we could handle.

We had considered two bags of birds—five per bag—a good catch heretofore. Now we kept running back to the truck for another bag, and still another. Os and Mary and Frederick and I rushed from trap to trap in the gathering dusk, and when night fell we found ourselves shouting to each other, "Have you got all the *bags* of birds?!"

We processed that big catch and then, weary and ecstatic, we drove home to light the fire in the big stove and warm up the stew. It had been a good day.

(*above*) PRAIRIE CHICKEN IS REMOVED FROM TRAP. (*above right*) NO MORE THAN FIVE CHICKENS PER BAG. (*right*) THE BIRD IS WEIGHED AND BANDED.

Normal operating procedure was rather different. Ordinarily we each ran a trapline about thirty miles long, twice a day. We covered as much ground as we could by car and snowshoed the rest. For some obscure reason it took us awhile to realize that big catches are often made during a thaw, rather than when the temperature is really low. However, it didn't take us long to learn that when the temperature drops right after a thaw and your clothes get wet, you get colder than you do in powdery snow.

That first year I had my own car, a used and battered telephone repairman's truck; and I made a pretty good catch alone. The rules of the project were in one respect inflexible. Never handle a chicken with gloves. Take off your mittens and use your bare hands. And there is good reason for this. The feathers of their drumsticks come off very easily; it was just common sense not to release bare-legged birds in the dead of winter. Bare fingers don't pull feathers out.

My catch was not enormous, but the thaw had just turned to a

THE BANDED CHICKEN IS RELEASED

good sharp freeze and my wet hands had taken on a bit more cold than I realized. I could hardly wait to get into the cab of my truck with the bags of birds, start the motor, and warm up. My teeth chattered, and my soggy clothes increased what we now call the chill factor. Thank heavens we'd never heard that demoralizing expression in those days!

I put the bags of birds on the floor of the cab and tried to turn the key to start the motor but my fingers couldn't manage to move it, so I slipped both hands inside my clothes next to the skin of my stomach and waited. I tried again, but I couldn't seem to get my thumb and index finger to meet. I almost got the wind up. How often had I been told that one small mistake in cold weather can be the end of the line? I couldn't get my mouth down to turn the key, but after several tries I managed to turn it by using the knuckles of my index and middle fingers. The motor burst into a satisfactory roar. I processed the birds and went home to tell Frederick of my adventure. He examined my hands with concern. Suddenly, with all ten fingers working again, it didn't seem such a close shave anymore.

Packs of prairie chickens tend to attract predators. When hawks and owls behold traps full of prairie chickens, they make repeated attacks, causing the chickens to thrash about and injure themselves. Occasionally during the skirmish, the talons of a large raptor nail a chicken right through the netting.

We finally learned to cope. But for several winters, whenever we ran into this sort of trouble, we just gave up and moved the traps to another station. Just one hawk or owl, weighing less than four pounds, could force us to lug hundreds of pounds of equipment out of a good station. As we were generally trapping in somebody else's cornfield, we carried bags of our own corn to bait the traps with. Carrying corn into a cornfield is better than being accused of stealing. Os is an enormously powerful man, and I remember carrying four bags of corn—which is heavy—into a faraway cornfield with him, as well as twelve traps. It took several trips on snowshoes. I took one end of each load and he took the other, and I prided myself on not suggesting that we stop and rest. And then, when we had a good-sized trapping station baited and set, we found a snowy owl working that pack. The next day we moved all the traps out again. By mutual consent we didn't carry the bait back out too.

Most of the farmers soon respected us, for we worked at all sorts of odd hours. We knew that the worse the weather was, the better our catches were apt to be. And we always seemed to be hurrying. One farmer, mystified after watching Frederick and me set up a station, asked, "Is anybody *timing* you?"

We felt that the farmers really had it hard, having to milk cows every single day and night, and they thought we had it hard, working outside in all weathers. They were good to us, and we sometimes planned the end of the trapline so we could stop in and get warm in somebody else's kitchen before going home to our own cold house.

But one farmer had me really scared. Frederick dropped me off to pick up a catch, while he drove on to the next station. It was getting late in the day and we were behind schedule. I snowshoed into the cornfield where a huge farm dog was working our traps. He had already killed two chickens and was after more of the same kind of excitement. I got the birds out of the traps and put them into bags, at which point the dog decided that he wanted to bite *me*. It is very hard to do anything at all when holding two fluttering bags of chickens over one's head out of reach of a serious dog, and even harder to kick the dog away when encumbered by snowshoes on both feet. Snowshoes are considerably bigger than tennis racquets, and you can kick just once. After the kick there is no way of getting the snowshoe back onto the ground, and the only alternative is to fall down. If I kicked once and failed to intimidate that enormous dog, he had a chance at me sitting helpless in the deep snow. Furthermore, my main aim was to protect the prairie chickens in the two bags I was holding above my head. Prairie chickens weigh about two pounds apiece, and I had to snowshoe back to safety holding some twenty-two fluttering pounds above my head.

The dog was a bit off base out in the cornfield. I yelled and shouted orders at him like, "Lie down," and "Get out of here." I didn't dare shout, "Go home," because that is just where I was heading! I was heading for *his* home where Frederick was going to meet me.

Somehow I managed to get to the farmhouse, and the dog didn't really bite me until I was almost at the door. Somewhat frantically I banged on the door and was let in. I didn't like the looks of the place, and I didn't like the looks of the man who had let me in. I figured that was no place for a young woman to be: the choice was inside with the man or outdoors with the dog and my precious chickens.

"Your dog bit me." I said accusingly.

"Never bites nobody."

I laid the bags of chickens on his floor and drew up a leg of my wool pants. There was a good-sized rent in the pants and enough blood on my tender pale skin to convince anyone that his dog really had bitten me. But I hadn't helped my cause. He didn't seem to be looking at the wound. That lonely old man—I suppose now that he was about forty—looked at a graceful feminine leg suddenly exposed right in his kitchen and he leered.

The next half hour or so I was nasty. Good and frightened, but nasty. He tried to pat my hand and I yelled, "How dare you keep a dog like that! Wait till my husband comes and see what he says!"

I had visions of his chasing me round and round his kitchen table like a villain in a 1920 movie. Now that I look back on it, I still don't know how matters would have turned out if Frederick hadn't "saved me" by knocking on the door. I probably panicked too soon, but I wasn't used to visiting strange men with a three-day growth of stubble on their faces and having them call me "Dearie."

Don't you move a muscle

Ordinarily one writes a lot of letters to solicit help when something has gone *wrong*. In the spring of 1950 we were faced with a major crisis because everything had gone so well. We, with the help of Os and Mary Mattson, had put numbered colored bands on 298 prairie chickens! There was no earthly way that three project members, even with Mary's help, could possibly cover all the booming grounds on the study area to see where the winter-banded birds might turn up.

A few graduate students and friends had helped us in spring for years when we were on our first shoestring study, but this was the Big Time. We needed more eyes to read band numbers. I put ten thin pieces of paper and nine thin sheets of carbon paper into the typewriter and wrote a sort of "To whom it may concern" letter. It ran something like this: "Dear ____, We have an emergency. We have banded so many prairie chickens that we need help. Come if you can. We live in an ancient, somewhat primitive farmhouse without modern conveniences, but we have lots of room and, if need be, can supply food."

I ran this communication, complete with nine carbon copies, through the typewriter several times, stuffed the letters into 3-cent envelopes and mailed them to just about everybody I could think of who might come.

Over 100 people came. One flew in from New York and stayed six weeks. People came in trucks and Cadillacs, they arrived on motorcycles, and two boys hitchhiked from Illinois.

At any rate, there was never again a need to *invite* anybody to come and help with the prairie chickens: the word was out that it was exciting, demanding, and an experience not to be missed.

I agreed. I wanted everybody to get a chance to watch the prairie chickens boom; there is nothing like it.

ANOTHER BUNCH OF BOOMERS

Frederick agreed too, but he soon said, ''I don't want more than ten observers at a time, and I want the best ones at the peak of the season when the hens come in.''

Little by little I developed a fair knack for segregating the best observers from the others: professional wildlifers tended to be very good, veterans of World War II were better than bird-watchers, high schoolers were mostly too young; and some ancient individuals of both sexes, wearing trifocals, kept good notes and read bands accurately.

On the other hand, not all presidents of big companies had a knack for reading bands and one gentleman, Allen Slichter, was membership chairman of the Society of Tympanuchus Cupido Pinnatus, one of the foundations to save prairie chickens. He flatly stated, ''I'll get you plenty of the right sort of members, but I absolutely refuse to get up early in the morning to get into one of those blinds to watch the prairie chickens.'' His contributions to the Society were invaluable.

In some respects the Society of Tympanuchus Cupido Pinnatus reminds me of President Truman's daughter's wedding: she invited only 600 intimate friends!

(Not everybody can get into the Society. Somewhat diffidently, but eager to buy more land for the prairie chickens, I once proposed a chap who was said to have lots of money, but gangster connections. My suggestion was turned down with a resounding "No.")

But I digress from the selection of good observers for peak seasons. They were selected in January each year. People had asked for booming season dates throughout the year, so I soon let it be known that reservations would not be made earlier. In January I placed a large calendar on my work table and sorted out the letters. (I always felt rather a fraud, as the calendar was still empty.) I started with Mrs. G., whose daughter-in-law has a hummingbird feeder, and who is looking for a home for her darling kittens, and who wants to come. Her stationery is pink and strongly scented (prairie chickens can't smell) and she says she would like to bring a camera.

"Hum," I said to myself, looking at the calendar. "She is plainly old, or she wouldn't have a daughter-in-law, and I'm not at all sure that she can take cold weather well. It would be heartless to put her into late March or early April. Making observations in early May is not apt to be demanding." I write:

Dear Mrs. G.,
Fortunately we have an opening on May 4 and would be delighted to have you come to watch the prairie chickens and help with our observations. Please bring a sleeping bag, warm clothes, and hip boots. We will expect you at 7:30 P.M. on May 3. Please let me know promptly if this is not satisfactory.

That accomplished, I write "Mrs. G." on the calendar. The first "boomer" of the season has been assigned.

The next letter is from the chief of the Research Section of the Wisconsin Conservation Department, our own bunch. I don't even have to think. They are the very best, and I put them down for April 19–20, the most important dates of the season.

Bill Brooks wants to bring a class from Ripon. He brought an unruly city-type boy once, but only once. I check the calender again. April 17 and 18 are also important dates.

Then I pull out a scribbled note: "Fran, I have a bunch of Cub Scouts and I really want them to see the chickens." Harry Croy has conned me into letting children in again. He is a good Scout leader, and kids can take the cold well.

83

Dear Harry,

You and your scouts may come on April 2. They will need plenty of warm clothes. Tell them it's going to be colder than sitting in a duck blind.

So it went. Year after year I wrote personal letters to each applicant.

Mrs. G. came and was much younger than I expected a mother-in-law to be and also far plumper than I had envisioned her. She arrived the year that we had a pet flying squirrel.

Dan Berger, the new project assistant, our daughter Elva, and I had captured a flying squirrel coming out of a hole in a popple, and I'm sure we only managed to catch her because she was a bit slow and very pregnant.

She gave birth to young in Berger's mother's garage. One of the young squirrels grew up in our house. This endearing pet was terrified of company. It had several hiding places and it was always at home on a member of the household, to whom it could glide from tops of doors or bookcases to hide beneath a warm shirt.

Mrs. G. came earlier than she was supposed to. As it happened I was cooking supper and I saw her legs cross the cracked, tilting cement of our back stoop: well-turned calves and somewhat swollen ankles in nylon stockings. She was short and wearing high heels.

She knocked on the back door and I continued frying onions with canned tomatoes to pour over the hamburgers, for the hungry crew was assembling. I just shouted, "Come in."

Mrs. G. opened the door with that falsely timid smile that most of us put on when nobody welcomes us correctly at the door of a strange house. After that everything happened quickly.

Mrs. G. took one step into the kitchen. The flying squirrel, atop the kitchen cabinet, panicked at the sound—or possibly the scent—of a stranger. Mrs. G. felt a rat-sized mammal scrabble down the front of her pink knit dress and claw its way inside her bra.

Mrs. G. yelped, then screamed. She started to beat and claw at her chest with both hands. Berger and Socha, both sturdy outdoor men with big black beards, jumped to save the squirrel. Mrs. G. felt herself seized and pinned against the door of the refrigerator. When she was satisfactorily immobilized, Berger, who was wearing a hideous pair of yellow sunglasses that made his six foot three inches even more sinister, commanded, "Stand perfectly still. Don't you move a muscle."

Berger has a way with animals. I stopped cooking and got him half a pecan. He tightened his grip on Mrs. G.'s shoulder, roughly commanding, "Don't you dare move." Suddenly his voice was gentle. "It's OK." He made soft clucking noises by gently clicking his tongue against the roof of his mouth and simultaneously he tapped the base of Mrs. G.'s throat with the pecan. "Cluck, cluck, cluck, tap, tap, tap." In a moment the squirrel scratched its way upward and dove inside Berger's shirt with the pecan.

Leaving Mrs. G. to her own devices in the vicinity of the refrigerator, we all followed Berger into the living room and watched anxiously as he checked the squirrel over for possible injuries.

At last I went back to my cooking. Mrs. G. was still standing by the refrigerator, holding on to it with one hand.

"It's all right," I said pouring tomato and onion sauce over the hamburger, "You didn't hurt it at all."

The following January I received a nice letter from Mrs. G.—again on pink, scented paper. "Please give me a date to watch the prairie chickens and if not too inconvenient for you, I would like to bring two friends."

Harry's Cub Scouts

Essentially everything we did was connected with the prairie chickens—but not quite everything: we were never able to squelch our interest in the birds of prey. Officially, Frederick was working full time for the Conservation Department, but I supposedly worked only 60% of the time so if the children came down with measles or something of the sort I would have plenty of time to nurse them. Actually we worked almost every waking hour, but my 40% free time gave my conscience a rest when I went loping about the marsh catching and banding hawks and owls. I always figured if I wanted to spend my free time playing bridge, it was my right to do so, and if I happened to prefer trapping hawks, that too was my right. The department more than got its money's worth from me.

I did, however, have to be careful about public relations. To put it more simply: it was up to me to avoid criticism. In those days hawks and owls were considered "vermin." It would have been better public relations to catch them and wring their necks than to put bands on them and let them go. At that time Portage County still paid a bounty on marsh hawks, which had been protected by the state for some time.

My solution was to keep a low profile. I hid my traps from the public, and when I went to check them I ambled across the meadows as though going nowhere special, when I really wanted to run to see if I'd made a catch. I also took advantage of just about any quick opportunity to catch a hawk.

One day when I was driving home after moving blinds from one booming ground to another, I spotted a red-tailed hawk perched on the far side of a pasture. The gate was open, so without a moment's hesitation I swung into the meadow and reached simultaneously for a baited trap. It's not too bad to drive on a frozen pasture without permission, but to my dismay my wheels cut through the sod; a low spot lay directly in my way and I gunned the motor to ram the car through

86

without getting stuck. Mud and sod hurtled on either side of the car. First the front wheels hit a depression and then the rear wheels fell into the hole and stopped. It would take a tractor to get me out. The redtail was long gone. Dejectedly, I walked to the nearest farm for help.

The farmer was very pleasant, until he found out *whose* field I was stuck in. The trail of destruction left by my tracks on the field was beyond belief. He hitched up a chain and pulled my car out backwards. And the huge treads of his tractor almost dwarfed the damage I had done.

"Look at that! Just look what you've done!"

I picked up a sod in my bare hands and placed it carefully back in a rut. This pitiful attempt to right matters caused him to ask me one more anguished question before he drove away. "Who's going to put all that back?"

"I am. I'll see that it's done."

Such a silly statement depressed him more than ever.

"I *promise*. I promise it will be all right by noon tomorrow."

I thought I heard a little snort before the roar of the tractor motor drowned out further conversation. He didn't believe me.

Harry Croy has an absolute flair for breaking rules at the right time. Not only did he bring those Cub Scouts, but he brought more of them than we expected—and he brought them the only time I really needed them.

Shortly before noon the following day the farmer, who was "just going by," stopped his tractor. The field must have seemed covered with small, gnome-like children busily patting down the remaining little unevennesses with their little hands. The field I had desecrated was now again a smooth, even green.

He watched for quite awhile and then he turned his tractor around and drove back home.

He had something to tell his wife.

The funnel trap and boop, boop, boop

Even present-day research projects sometimes fall flat on their faces because the investigators haven't the foggiest notion how to catch and mark the animals they are working on.

Aldo Leopold used to say trapping seems to lie in the blood. Our blood was that of seafarers. Frederick's ancestors were Vikings, and I am said to be a direct descendant of Captain Flint, the pirate. Maybe both our ancestors illegally captured lovely ladies from foreign ships, but this hardly seems the best inheritance for knowing how to trap the wily prairie hen—especially as the cocks are easier to catch.

Sometimes, when rather shy neighbors drop in and conversation becomes difficult, Frederick and I argue with some gusto which is better: his Vikings or my pirates. It tends to break the ice. We avoid the discussion of trapping. Once a trapping discussion is started we simply forget that anyone else is in the house.

We have built hundreds of traps and devised and/or modified dozens of designs. We have caught more prairie chickens in funnel traps than in any other device. At first we tried the then standard tall and narrow funnels, and the prairie chickens walked in and out of them as though they were doors made specially for entrance *and* exit. Broad, sloppy funnels made of unreinforced chicken wire were far better than the standard, tidy, rigid funnels we first devised. Once a prairie chicken is caught and has eaten its cropful of bait, it tends to walk the edge of the inside of the trap, now and again trying to get out through the soft netting with which the trap is covered. Round and round they go and, in theory, each time they come to a funnel they walk up over it. Soft, floppy, unreinforced funnels soon mash down so that they work like self-shutting doors.

Of course we had read the old books and articles in *Forest and Stream* to learn how to trap chickens. The old-timers had found trapping so easy that our industrious efforts were put to shame. They often used a tip-top trap, set in a cornfield, and they had to empty it frequently. This sounded like an easy method for getting the winter's meat supply, and surely we could adapt it for banding.

It is great fun to watch a prairie chicken land on top of the trap, prepared to eat ear corn, and watch him slide unwillingly down into the trap. He can't take off and fly as he cannot possibly regain his footing; his footing is falling away from him every time his feet, more or less running backward, add to the speed of his descent into the trap. In less than a minute he is inside and the counterweight has moved the top of the trap back up, ready for the next innocent bird.

What wasn't fun was that we couldn't tack the netting onto the trap loosely enough so that the birds wouldn't injure themselves occasionally. To solve this problem, we covered the traps with burlap, knowing that chickens would not struggle in the dark. This innovation ran afoul too. The slightest bit of wind caused the traps to drift solid full of snow. We soon learned that the real trick was not just to catch birds, but to catch them without hurting them.

What we learned from the old books about trapping was simply irritating. What we learned from them about the temperament of prairie chickens was utterly frustrating.

My envy borders on rage whenever I look at a picture of prairie chickens happily sitting about on the backs of chairs in the kitchen of an early settler, while some woman in a long skirt stirs a pot on the stove. I want to be that woman! Frederick is perfectly content observing wild animals (preferably individually marked) in their natural state. I am not.

My mind has an ethological bent and I wanted to live with prairie chickens as companions. I wanted them to come when I called, but in general I wanted them to have their being quite naturally—indoors and out—without their paying any particular attention to me. I have managed such relationships with eagles, hawks, owls, mice, squirrels, foxes, raccoons and—with some degree of success—with green herons.

When a storm is about to burst, it is not uncommon for various creatures to scratch on doors or sit on window sills waiting to be let *into* our house. No prairie chicken has even indicated that it wanted this privilege.

I realized that my best chance to tame prairie chickens was to start with newly hatched chicks, and Frederick gave me every possible opportunity to acquire some. Each time we found a nest that had been doomed by a mowing machine, I held the eggs close to the skin next to my stomach while Frederick drove me swiftly to the nearest setting domestic hen, or—more often—back to our house. Hatchability of prairie chicken eggs is excellent; those chicks are determined to come out of the shell. I have even brought off a hatch in the oven of our old kerosene stove with the burners turned way down. And later, after we put in electricity, I got a little incubator, and brought off another splendid hatch of fine, lively chicks. They followed me about on the lawn, and my happiness was so great that I could barely leave them long enough to cook for the family.

They didn't seem to want to eat much, so I put them in a nice warm container with plenty of light and offered wild strawberries, grated egg yolk, and hundreds of living insects.

Prairie chickens differ from domestic chickens in the way they rear their young. The domestic hen tends to lead her brood, and the chicks watch her pick at this and that. They appear to follow her example. The prairie hen, on the other hand, keeps her chicks from getting too far apart by calling them from time to time, but other than that it is my impression that her young are out of control in that they eat what they please and learn to do it all by themselves by trial and error.

The prairie chicks I hatched in an incubator had no sense for eating anything. They followed me after a fashion, came when I called, "Boop, boop, boop," but they almost entirely neglected to eat. Like

PART OF THE PACK AT DUSK

(George P. Koshollek, Milwaukee Journal)

all the other prairie chicks I tried to hand-rear, most died on the second or third day of life after their nutritious little yolk sacs had been absorbed; their sibs gradually weakened and died over a period of about two weeks.

A few people have successfully reared prairie chickens. Hurst Shoemaker in Illinois reared a substantial number, and some of the cocks grew up and displayed to him as though he were a hen; Arnold Kruse reared an astonishing number in North Dakota in the 1970s. One chap dipped living mealworms in batter for food and even raised prairie chickens in battery brooders—those trays that domestic chickens, destined to become fryers, grow up in.

My friend, Pat Ware, once said to me, "If Fran Hamerstrom had lived 300 years ago she would have been burned as a witch, for her way with wild animals is uncanny."

She was right only in part; I have failed in the one species I most wanted to work with as a companion. Furthermore I'm glad that I'm living right now. I can very often figure out just what almost any wild animal needs or wants without really putting my mind on it, it's usually just obvious to me and I find the thought of being burned as a witch repugnant.

I never relinquished my dream of living with a tame prairie chicken. Now and again an acquaintance would send us a newspaper clipping about a prairie cock who inhabited an airport and displayed on the wings of the planes, or of a filling station attendant who could throw his hat toward a prairie cock and this bird—showing the close bond that I had hoped to establish—displayed to the hat.

These reports invariably reached us weeks, months, or years after those eccentric cocks were no longer displaying or were dead. If I could only get current reports!

One day when I was washing my hair in a bowl of hot water on the kitchen floor, the telephone rang. It was a game warden. "There's a prairie chicken down here in Marquette County that's hooked on a manure spreader. It follows it around all the time."

I pushed my long, wet hair out of my eyes and shouted into the receiver, "Can you catch it?"

"I've already caught it. I put it in a chicken coop. I think it's *lonely.*"

Maybe that warden should have been burned as a witch too, because I think he was dead right. I ignored details and shouted into the receiver, "Can you catch it again and get it to us?"

People's reactions to the Hamerstrom household vary, but are almost always extreme. Some have said that the conditions are perfectly appalling; and others, in a tone of reverence, have soberly stated that they never felt nearer to God.

I figured that a prairie cock that had fallen in love with a manure spreader might find our ménage a happy home.

I moved our bed out of the north porch, where we usually sleep in summer, and installed pine boughs for cover. The cock, magnificently healthy, arrived aflutter in a burlap bag, and I released him in our summer bedroom (Frederick was very nice about it).

I have no idea how many hours I spent with that cock. I read in his presence and slept in his presence and spent every free moment in his presence. Not once did he mistake me for his manure spreader.

Then I decided to get tough. That bird was fed corn and other grains, but I withheld protein. If he wanted protein he had to come to me for it. Day after day I dropped squirming earthworms on the floor of the porch and called, "Boop, boop, boop."

He learned to rush toward me for those goodies if I stood very still, but I got to feeling more like Simon Legree than a companion. Finally, reluctantly, I gave up. I netted him, banded him, and released him in our garden.

The next day I called, "Boop, boop, boop." There was no response. I never saw him again.

Had I had sense enough to go to Marquette County myself and record the sound of the manure spreader, I could have played the sound back to him. Perhaps he would have come flying from afar to put in among my pansies and lilacs. He might even have followed me into the house and caused my cup to run over: he might have perched on one of my kitchen chairs.

Try as I might, I never succeeded in making that bird happy, but I have some small consolation: never have I made my man unhappy by playing the sound of a manure spreader right inside our house. Frederick is musical—and his hearing is far more acute than mine.

The love life of the prairie hen

The love life of the prairie hen lasts about five days each year. After most of the cocks have established territories and boomed for a month or more, the first hen is apt to appear on the booming ground. The moment she arrives the cocks near her increase the intensity of their booming. Their huge orange air sacs are blown up like distorted balloons. The cocks beat a rapid tattoo with their feet and move around the hen like mechanical toys. And there is a new sound on the booming ground—the "ladies present" call, which sounds rather like the high, clear honk of the Canada goose.

Those cocks that are unfortunate enough *not* to have the hen near them cackle in excitement and "flutter jump." The flutter jump is far different from the majestic beauty of a booming cock. Flutter-jumping cocks fly awkwardly almost straight up into the air as though crippled and come more or less tumbling down only to cackle and flutter jump again, no doubt in order to attract the hen. (Cocks

THESE HENS ARE INDIFFERENT

(*above*) A FLIRTATIOUS HEN

(*below left*) A RECEPTIVE HEN

(*below*) THE TRIUMPHANT MOMENT

do not flutter jump when a hen is near; they already have one!) The first day that a prairie hen visits a booming ground she appears *indifferent*. Her behavior is almost indistinguishable from that of a hen wandering about in a meadow all by herself! She appears to ignore all the wild excitement she has generated and seems to wander about on the booming ground at random. She picks at willow buds and such, but this is not real eating; it's substitute behavior, like a lecturer pulling at his ear when he doesn't know what to say next. When Day 1 is past, *indifference* is over.

On Day 2 the hen has undergone a subtle change: she is *aware*. She walks the booming ground, moving through the territory of each cock. She was courted yesterday but is courted even more intensively now, and it is perfectly plain—even to a person—that she is aware. She reacts without taking initiative. As many as four cocks may boom around her in what I've called the "Indian War Dance." She holds up her long slender neck, declaring her femininity: a simple statement—nothing more.

On Day 3 she is *flirtatious*. She has developed a quick little wing flick, and she tends to run away from each courting cock—but she never runs very far. After all, she has the power of flight and could

95

easily just fly away from the booming ground. A flirtatious hen stays right close to those cocks. And by now she is staying right close to certain cocks; she may have singled one out.

On Day 4 the hen has reached the *seductive* stage. Her movements are slower and more deliberate; she spreads her wings wide in invitation, but she still runs away. Each time she runs from a cock, she runs a very short distance. Now white feathers may appear near the shoulder. These are excitement spots.

We suspect that excitement spots are an adrenalin reaction—like hair standing up on a cat's back—and we also suspect that the prairie chickens themselves are unaware of the excitement signal. We have seen these excitement spots appear under three different circumstances: just before a big fight (in cocks), just before copulation, and sometimes just before death.

As far as we have been able to detect, excitement spots are of no practical value to prairie chickens. They are of enormous practical value to a wildlife photographer: he knows precisely which bird to focus on.

On Day 5 the hen has at last reached the *receptive* stage. She may arrive on the booming ground still in the seductive stage, but each time she spreads her wings in invitation and crouches, she holds the invitation a little longer—sometimes so long that the cock actually places his foot on her back, but if she isn't ready, she scoots out from under. When she is completely ready, she holds, and the cock mounts.

A prairie hen is never forced. Rape, so to speak, is unknown. The prairie hen is mounted when she is receptive, and not until she is good and ready.

This sequence—indifferent, aware, flirtatious, seductive, and receptive—has some variations but it is typical of the many banded hens we have known in over twenty-five years of watching booming grounds essentially every morning throughout the entire spring.

We didn't find out all these things alone. We had help from about 7,000 miscellaneous observers.

In some ways the notes we expected from them were simplified. For example, we didn't expect observers to follow the path of any given hen, and certainly not to follow the kaleidoscopic paths of sixteen or so hens walking one booming ground simultaneously, some aware, some seductive, etc. And to further confuse the picture, the hens may put on a sister act and stick together like a bunch of giggling girls downtown on a Saturday night.

We spared most observers this welter of confusion and, as far as

96

hens were concerned, just asked them to count them, record their band numbers, whether or not copulation occurred, with which cock, and was it successful?

Every evening after the new arrivals put their duffle on their bunks, we held a briefing for the ten to fourteen observers going out into the blinds the next morning. The questions asked about hens were all straightforward and needed no explanation except the one about successful copulation. If a cock mounts a hen and makes contact before getting knocked off by another cock, and the hen "rouses"—shakes her feathers violently—and if the cock thereupon tears off to fight or intimidate another cock, and the hen leaves the booming ground within ten minutes, the copulation was successful. It is *that* hen's last visit to the booming ground and time for her to reprogram her body for egg-laying. Sometimes, a month or so after a successful copulation, we have seen a banded hen return and have assumed that her eggs had been broken.

Theoretically, the territorial system should prevent conflict and make for uninterrupted copulations, but over and over again, the immediate vicinity of a seductive hen became a jumble like the pile-up on a football field. Even professionals had trouble taking good notes.

Ordinarily, I preferred to be by myself every morning, but when Colonel Nial Rankin, husband of the Chief Lady-in-Waiting of the Queen of England, came to watch the prairie chickens, I volunteered to let him share my blind, hoping to learn about the doings in the palace. He proved to be an outstanding observer. To my amazement, he read every band number correctly with my scope whilst mumbling, "Magnificent equipment you have . . . magnificent." It appeared he was too shy to talk, so I told him about the love life of the prairie hen.

I learned nothing about the palace, but when it came time to wash the huge stack of dishes we had accumulated I heard a cultivated voice inquire, "Couldn't I help you?"

I tossed him a dish towel, which he caught dexterously, and soon I learned a bit about what I assume was the attitude toward dishes in the palace. He wiped the top of each dish, then he wiped its bottom, then he carried it across the kitchen and held it up to the window to make sure that both the top and the bottom of it gleamed—after which he walked back across the kitchen and placed it in the cabinet, as though it were the egg of an extinct bird.

It was plain that it would take all morning to get the dishes wiped at this rate, but just as I was about to yell for another wiper, the colonel gave a dry little British cough and said, "Maybe I shouldn't tell this one, but Her Majesty was amused. . . ."

I had no idea the British told stories like that! I listened to one after another, laughing and astounded.

The Queen was one up on me: she was amused by a story I didn't understand at all, and it *did* take all morning to get the dishes done.

The Second Breakfast

The Second Breakfast was the high social point of the day. There was no hurry. Some very fine amateur chefs have cooked the Second Breakfast, but usually I served a big tray of toasted cheese sandwiches (if you pass around just an ordinary tray somebody is sure to say "thank you," put it on his lap, and start eating, thinking they are all for him!).

After the cold hours in the blinds the warmth of the big stove—and for some of the novices, perhaps the sheer relief of having gotten back safely—made for a merry, noisy atmosphere. Frederick brought in more coffee one day, as a big black man in a cream sheep-lined coat accepted another sandwich. I noticed his accent was British. "Astounding, Mrs. Hamerstrom. Such fighting ability! Your prairie chickens are astounding. Where can I buy some?"

"You want to *buy* some prairie chickens?" Fencing for time, I stammered, "Where do you live?"

"Jamaica." He explained, "I simply must take some back with me to cross with my fighting cocks."

"I'm afraid it's not practical." Across the room a wispy little girl was trying to pull off *my* hip boots. "Would you mind helping that girl pull off those boots?"

The magnificent gentleman from Jamaica crossed the room, introduced himself to the small, startled freshman with a charming little bow. She grabbed both arms of the red chair, and leaned back. He knelt to ease the first boot off: a pool of muddy water formed on the floor. He eased the second boot off: a larger puddle ran out of that one, spreading over the boards and down into the cracks.

I gave my friend from Jamaica a broad grin—approving a job well done. Then I lent the girl my fur-lined moccasins to warm up her skinny, white feet.

I owned *two* pairs of hip boots and almost never got to wear them myself! And Frederick bought himself a brand new pair of rubber boots one year; he never got to wear them once all booming season. Our boots, our parkas, our mittens, were worn by others day after day. So few people followed instructions and brought the right clothes . . . and we were toughened to wind, icewater wet feet, and the raging spring storms of central Wisconsin.

It had been a good morning. But there were sixteen boomers and only two of us to check their notes. The dirty dishes left over from the First Breakfast were hidden under the kitchen stove. Time to get to work.

The purpose of the Second Breakfast was not purely social: it was our chance to check everyone's notes and straighten out any confusion in band numbers, etc. If people just left their notes with us we often had to hound them for weeks by mail to answer questions that they couldn't even answer anymore.

We had dawdled long enough. It was 9:30. We had already worked seven hours and wanted to get to bed by 10:00. I looked across the room at Frederick. He hadn't been dawdling; I had. I'd been telling people stories about prairie chickens, quite forgetting that we were short-handed! Frederick had been checking notes and looking up band numbers for heaven only knows how long.

I seized the nearest boomer by the wrist and asked, "Have your notes been checked?"

"Er, no."

We settled down with his notes. Sixteen cocks and eleven hens. I got up to compare with a big pile of other notes from the same booming ground. He had all the band numbers right on the cocks, but he missed the hybrid.

"Anything funny about that cock way over to the left?"

"Funny about it?"

I set his map of territories in front of him. "Here's green 23, the one that sometimes comes and fights right in front of the blind." He nodded. "And then there's the unbanded one who fights with him." He agreed again. "And off to the side and a little farther away, there's this one. Anything funny about this one?"

The boomer looked at me as though I were psychic and asked very slowly, "How did you *know?*"

"Tell me about him."

"You can see where I kept erasing. Sometimes I was sure he was a hen because his neck tufts were too short, but then he boomed!"

"Good observation. That's the hybrid cock—a cross between a prairie chicken and a sharp-tailed grouse."

I initialed his notes and reached for somebody else's.

Frederick appeared unexpectedly, "There are two cars still out, and you'd better have a look in the kitchen."

I put down the notes and rushed into the kitchen. "Oh, no!" I moaned. Somebody had found the dirty dishes, piled my grandmother's lovely silverware in with the aluminum cooking utensils, and was adding boiling soapy water. "Silver can't be washed with aluminum. It ruins the patina." I poured a bucket of cold water into the dishpan, fished the silver out quickly, and stored everything back under the stove. "Thank you for offering to help, but somebody will come to do them." It was one of my better white lies. I didn't add that the "somebody" would be the two Hamerstroms.

"Now where were we?" I asked settling back to checking notes.

"You were just starting."

I looked at "arrival time of birds." His birds arrived nine minutes late. "What time is it?"

His watch was nine minutes behind. "Did you synchronize your watch with Dr. Hamerstrom's last night?"

"No, was I supposed to?"

"Maybe nobody told you. OK, fourteen cocks and two unbanded hens. Are you sure both hens were unbanded? Could you tell for certain?"

There was a sound in the kitchen I didn't much like, so I put the notes down to take a look. The would-be dishwasher was standing guiltily by the refrigerator. "I was just putting the butter away."

I took the butter dish from her gently and said, "We leave it at room temperature so it will spread."

"Now," settling down to the notes again, "could you see both legs of both hens?"

101

Frederick, who does not like to raise his voice and prefers to walk quietly across a room to ask a question, called, "Fran, where are yesterday's notes from Hakes booming ground?"

To his surprise I didn't shout back. I pushed my way through the throng and whispered, "They were absolutely no good. I burned them."

"I've spent at least twenty minutes looking for those notes." His voice was beginning to lose its timbre from sheer lack of sleep.

I added, "I'm sorry, I should have told you."

Suddenly a great clatter of new, happy voices moved from the back door into the living room. The lost carloads had finally arrived! What a relief. At any rate we wouldn't have to go out to the marsh to look for them. But it was harder to settle down and check the remaining notes with the newcomers telling everybody what they had just seen. I made toasted cheese sandwiches for them and heated up more coffee.

When I got back to the living room I saw Frederick with his shoulders hunched up trying to check the notes of a gray-haired man in a plaid shirt. He was deliberately ignoring a rather large woman in a beige knitted dress who kept trying to attract his attention.

"Dr. Hamerstrom," she exclaimed, "I saw the dance of the hens!"

"*Tell* him," I shouted across the room, "*Tell* him about the dance of the hens!"

Encouraged by my enthusiasm, she raised her elbows and tripped in a semicircle in front of Frederick's chair on her plump feet.

Frederick's fists clenched and he threw me his worst Chief Thundercloud look. He thought I had picked this unfortunate moment to have some fun!

The moment that marvelous woman raised her "wings" and went into her dance, I knew that for the first time ever, the dance of the hens had been observed, because I had seen the same hen. "What time did you see it?" The lady and I compared times. The dancing hen—and we never saw another like her—danced in front of that lady and then she flew to my booming ground and danced in front of me.

Losing sleep over dancing hens is very worthwhile.

(Hugh Wilmar)

Can you trust 7,000 observers?

In some ways Frederick and I were naive when we started working on chickens; in other ways we were not. We started right out trying to distinguish between good, accurate observers and the other kind. Later we had plenty of ways of finding out. Every observer had to turn in his field notes, so we soon knew the band numbers, colors, and positions of all the regular cocks on each booming ground. After all, we built up a whole series of maps of each booming ground, detailing even minor changes in the positions of some of the cocks. *But* it was harder to read the band numbers of the hens; they seemed to spend a lot of time hunkering in the weeds, they might visit more than one booming ground, and besides, each hen's total days on a booming ground tend to be only five in all! You can be sure that we put what we hoped were the best observers where we expected the most hens!

After each evening's briefing we brought in red wine and had a discussion period. It was during the discussion period that Frederick—or whoever gave the briefing—had to make up his mind. The best observers had to be put on the key booming grounds. The decisions were always difficult to make because *we cared so intensely*. We wanted the data.

103

I'd look at a group of brand new faces: There is Ed Peartree. He's blind in one eye, but I think he has what it takes. (Right: he was one of our top observers for some nineteen years.)

And that chap Brown doesn't seem very well coordinated. I'll put him in a blind with me as a recorder. (Wrong: Brown kept up with me—almost running—and made it into the Lauritzen booming ground before the chickens got there, and his observations were perfect. I didn't learn until a year or two later that he had an artificial leg!)

We tended to discount the abilities of females, but some of these proved us very wrong. Marie McCabe (Mrs. R. A.) could sit in a blind, with those dreamy Madonna eyes of hers, and could read the numbers and colors of prairie chicken hens that came onto the booming ground in the half-light of the early dawn—and again and over again she was proved right. She'd catch the bands of those hens on Day 1 of their love life and give us a chance to follow up on the whole sequence.

Eventually we set up some ground rules: professional wildlifers were top of the heap. Hunters had quick eyes and an uncanny knack for reading band numbers. Presidents of large companies were far more accustomed to giving orders than to taking them and did not really pay attention to instructions very well. I remember one: Frederick was giving the briefing that evening and I heard him say, "Your notes will be taken in pencil."

An egregiously distinguished-looking gentleman, with well-brushed silvery hair and a commanding deep golden voice, replied, "I always take notes with this gold pen. It was given me by the President of the United States."

Frederick brushed this comment off as though it were a fly buzzing about his scrambled eggs at breakfast. "You will use pencil!" Almost as an afterthought, but governed by innate courtesy, he added, "Ink freezes."

However we may have failed to sort the good observers from the rest during the briefing, we would know with certainty how we had fared when the notes came in at the end of the morning: we could trust the notes of those who had made a good map of the territories and read all the cock bands correctly. No one went home before his notes had been checked, and the originals stayed with us. New boomers had no idea that we had such an efficient cross check on their observations!

Poor observers sometimes simply couldn't see well enough. Other poor observers we lumped among the prudes: they tended to

BRIEFING

behave in a silly, rather suggestive manner and, when pinned down, were forced to admit that they had observed a copulation.

Another group was the suggestible. One evening during the discussion period someone asked me if we had wolves on the study area. I told them about the only two times we had seen coyotes, members of the wolf family, on a booming ground. Here are my field notes: *"The coyotes came in from the north and worked the whole booming ground. They behaved like sheep looking for vegetation, rather than prairie wolves a-hunting. Slowly they walked around the whole booming ground and one after another, each cock was flushed. Then one coyote came right up to the blind. His eyes were within inches of mine and I suddenly realized, 'This is, after all, a wolf' and became uneasy. Then the coyotes sat to watch the show. Two coyotes and I watched the prairie chickens display. It was a grand moment. Then the coyotes loped off . . . and disappeared.*

"I saw the coyotes once more, the very next day, but the wind was wrong. Both of them scented me; it was as though they tripped over an invisible wire. They just took off." I had found my experiences with the coyotes mighty fascinating, but I didn't expect my description of these two, long ago mornings to brainwash one third of the boomers at the briefing!

When the notes came in the next morning, coyotes had been seen from *three* different blinds! Frederick was aghast. So was I, but I had a good idea of what was up. I practically battled with the boomers who insisted that they had seen coyotes. One backed down right quick and honorably admitted that all he had seen was a sort of shadow that might have been a farm dog or something. However, the other two stuck with their coyote stories.

Twice in twenty-five years of chicken watching have coyotes been seen. Once, during a briefing, were coyotes vividly described. Thrice were coyotes reported by boomers. Guess when? The morning after my vivid description!

So much for suggestibility.

There is a far worse problem: the outright liar who sticks to his lie. There fortunately aren't many of these people, but they cropped up from time to time. I kept waiting my chance to find out *why* people ever behave like this. We've spotted them off and on: they insist that they saw something that we know to be impossible. We have many ways of checking up on them without their knowing.

At last I had my chance! Just what I wanted. A professor of psychology arrived with his students, and the professor himself had some peculiar discrepancies in his notes: he had reported a pink and white spiral band (we have never used pink and white spiral bands) and he reported a three-digit number (we have never used three-digit numbers).

I asked one of the students to pass out the toasted cheese sandwiches so I could reread the professor's notes carefully. Some of his numbers and colors were impossible.

The professor, sitting on the bench beside me, lit his pipe and smoked quietly.

"I'd like to ask you about one of the birds. The cock with the pink and white spiral band on one leg and the number 357. How good was the light when you recorded this?"

"The light was fine." He answered easily.

"Was the sun already up?" I persisted.

"Yes, bright sunlight." The professor uncrossed his legs and appeared a little less relaxed.

"You're not color-blind are you?"

"I'm certainly not color-blind!"

Plainly, he was indignant at the very suggestion, so I added quickly, "I didn't think so. You got most of the colors right."

He relaxed a little.

"How far away from you was that bird?"

The professor answered, smiling and in a condescending tone.

"The bird was in perfectly plain sight and so near that I could see every detail. It was right in the middle of the booming ground all morning."

He started to get up to leave, but I said, "Just a minute. You see, I want to learn something. We have never used pink spirals and we never used three-digit numbers. Besides we know the colors and numbers of every cock on that booming ground.

"You're a psychologist," I continued delightedly, "I've been longing to ask a psychologist. Perhaps you can help me? Why do people report things that are impossible and then stick to them even after they have been proven wrong? Is it compulsive like kleptomania?

The professor knocked the ashes out of his pipe. "I was not wrong. I know what I saw."

"And you're absolutely sure?"

"Absolutely."

Somehow my golden opportunity to learn from a psychologist why people tell lies and stick to them slipped between my fingers. Perhaps it was my fault. I was too eager to learn the cause of this phenomenon to appreciate the plight of the poor professor surrounded by his students and caught in two outright lies.

He never came back.

On being helpful

Some boomers were forever helping each other or helping us. There was the time that "the Duke," a fellow graduate student and now a famous scientist, came up with Bob McCabe to watch the chickens. He brought 200 mousetraps with him and stated, "I want to set them in a creek bottom." We got to the creek bottom, baited the 200 mousetraps, and found ourselves setting all his traps for him while he sat under a large white oak. I figured he wasn't feeling well, but as soon as we got back to the house, he regaled us with stories about all the amusing things his black bearers had done in Africa. The rest of the men peeled potatoes, and I cut up some meat and onions for the mulligan. At last McCabe interrupted, "Why don't you help? Why don't you go pump some water, and while you're at it, take the slop pail out too."

As soon as the Duke was safely out of the house, I said, "Bob, I don't think he's feeling well."

McCabe picked up a long potato peel, leaned back, and fanned himself with it. Imitating the Duke's haughty intonation, he mimicked, "And when I snapped my fingers they came running; one built the fire, one unfolded the bathtub, and one beat a drum to chase away the evil spirits."

When the Duke came back into the house, McCabe was sprawled on his stool, cowering in mock terror from the evil spirits, and managing to keep the potato peel fan moving.

We tried not to laugh, and I thanked the Duke when he set the water pail down on the floor. Then I gasped, "What's in it?"

The water was dirty and had a bilious scum. Frederick was mystified, "Where'd the dirt and oil come from?"

The Duke drew himself up rather grandly and announced, "I suppose you know that one primes a pump."

McCabe was the first to take in the full enormity of what had happened. Fists clenched, he roared, "So you put on your thinking cap and primed the pump with the slop! Go pump till the water comes clean."

We took twenty-minute turns at pumping far into the night. It was a short night: breakfast was at 3:00 A.M.

We were always short of sleep during the booming season. With luck we got to bed by eleven. Frederick tended to get up at 2:30 A.M. and let me have twenty minutes extra sleep. With luck we got back into bed by 11:00 A.M.—sometimes even by 10:00—for our nap. Up again to eat, move blinds, fix equipment, and prepare for the next group of boomers. What with loss of sleep, excitement, cold, and all the stimulating people with whom we wanted to stay up, we lost ten pounds apiece on four meals a day each spring. Sleep was our most precious commodity; you don't just go to bed when there's work to be done or when some of the most fascinating biologists in the world are right in your living room expounding theories or telling yarns.

There are so many ways one can lose a nap. Tom Gilliard, from the American Museum of Natural History, came to watch the chickens and to bring back three or four boxes of prairie vegetation for a display case. Frederick, Dan Berger, and I all volunteered to dig the plants for him; but no, he had to hire a boy! He was *not* going to trouble us with any twenty-minute job. He wanted to hire a boy. That blew another nap. The high school couldn't find a boy, the grade school couldn't find a boy, and none of the neighbor boys were interested. At last I called Larry Crawford, also on the chicken project, and said, "Larry, can you do us a favor? I know it isn't your job, but could you just go dig up some plants for Dr. Gilliard?"

"Sure."

By then it was Larry's supper time, and he'd been working crazy hours too. That little job of digging up those plants had cost the Prairie Chicken Project at least six hours by sundown! We never did find a boy, and Gilliard never found out that it was Larry Crawford of the Game Management Division who dug up his plants!

Lack of sleep may have made me somewhat uncharitable to the helpful. Two well-dressed ladies drove in from Buffalo, New York, at 11:00 one morning, just as I was going to slip into bed. "We don't want to trouble you. We came a little early," they said in their nice, well-bred, Eastern voices. "Perhaps you could recommend a farmhouse that could put us up for the night?"

109

"You can stay right here. We have four guest rooms. You can take your pick of any two, or share one."

"No, my dear," the older lady pierced me with her firm blue eyes, and smiled. "We are *not* going to trouble you. Just a simple farmhouse?"

Throughout my childhood I had been trained not to argue with ladies of this very type—ladies from that other world I'd left so far behind. Even the intonation of their voices reminded me of my teachers and some of my more forceful aunts so I meekly spent my nap time telephoning our neighbors trying to find somebody who would take them in. Nobody wanted them. But Mrs. Cook, our neighbor to the north, had sounded uncertain, simply saying, "Why, Mrs. Hamerstrom, I don't think we could do anything like that!" She was worth another try.

At last—exasperated—I commanded the ladies, "You wait right here." Then I jumped into the car and roared into the Cooks' driveway. Mrs. Cook and I argued for almost an hour. Now and again Mr. Cook chipped in a word or two. Finally Mrs. Cook said, "Well maybe, . . ." and I exclaimed, "Thank you ever so much."

Finally—utterly exhausted—I tiptoed into the house hoping not to wake Frederick. The ladies were sitting quietly at our dining room table reading. There was a buzzing sound from the next room.

"What's that?" they asked anxiously.

"That," I answered bitterly, "is the alarm clock telling me it's time to get up"

110

I just don't know where *to spit*

My family not only dreamed about what their only daughter would do; they planned it. I was groomed to feel at home in the capitals of Europe and qualified to become the wife of an ambassador. The dream and the plan were that I would become an international hostess.

By a curious twist of fate I did become an international hostess, but instead of flitting about world capitals, I helped my husband entertain in quite a variety of abandoned farmhouses. The farmhouses—needless to say—were no longer abandoned after we moved into them, but never once did we move into a farmhouse that anyone had lived in recently, and we fixed them up the way we liked them, rather than conforming to the American standard of living.

Our house tends to be full of *"gabboons"*—a politer term would be apprentices.

The word gabboon, I have been told, was once spelled with a "C" and referred to a wretched African tribe, forced into slavery by a more powerful tribe—to be fed on scraps and to conduct low forms of labor.

Most of the gabboons are mine, and my loyalty toward them is strong. (Many, but not all, have gone on to distinguished careers.) In recent years I hardly know how to address the new crop because they are so much quieter and more polite than the earlier ones. In the early years they were a rowdy lot, and even I was appalled at some of their ways. One Christmas they brought us two turkeys wrapped in foil, which I popped into the oven and roasted. When we sat down to feast, Frederick, who was carving, gasped, "Fran, these birds aren't drawn! You cooked them with the guts in!"

"Why," I stammered, "they were wrapped in foil." Turning to the gabboons I asked, "Where did you buy them?"

"Buy them!" they howled. "We stole them!" And one added virtuously, "We plucked them for you."

111

Most of that rambunctious group had arrived in a beat-up old car, but three had hitch-hiked from Illinois. It had taken them two days. Knowing they had no money, I was mystified. I asked, "Where did you spend the night on the way?"

This simple question was greeted by beating on the chest and yelling. It appeared that some of the gabboons—determined to help us with our research—had developed the art of arranging for a free room just about any time. They explained, "It's simple. Stir up just enough trouble and a free bed is offered you—a nice warm room in a jail."

Six or eight might come for a weekend; more often there were only two or three, and these might live with us for months. As Frederick found their table manners distressing, I'd put a big bunch of flowers on the dinner table and seat the gabboon with the worst manners behind the bouquet. I used to pick a lot of flowers in those days.

As luck would have it, when our first distinguished European guest was about to arrive, we had a houseful of gabboons. I gave them a strict briefing. "Watch your table manners. Don't hunker over your food and gnaw on the bones. And don't wear undershirts at mealtime."

Tom Oar, a rodeo rider, deliberately mistaking my meaning by pretending that I was forbidding an undershirt under his shirt, asked, "What if it's cold?" He looked outdoors and managed a fake shiver.

"You know perfectly well what I mean. You don't have to wear ties," I shouted in a voice unbecoming to an international hostess. His brother Jack listened with interest, ready to take sides if need be. Blood sometimes flows when gabboons take sides.

I assembled all the gabboons, lowered my voice, and simply said, "Look, you idiots, this visit means an awful lot to me."

Then Gustav Kramer—the brilliant biologist who invented an artificial sun to study bird orientation—arrived, eager to pick up American expressions, especially slang.

Kramer asked, "How do you say *prosit* when everyone holds up his glass for drinking?"

"Here's mud in your eye!" I replied.

"People actually say *that?*"

"Yes."

Kramer tried this toast out on the gabboons that very same evening and was rewarded by a delighted respect. "And here's mud in yours!" they roared.

The next morning he asked, "How do you greet in the country? Do you say 'Hello' or 'Hi'?"

"You say, 'How are the chickens?'" I answered with a straight face.

"*That* is what is said in the United States?"

"Yes," I answered. "Look, I have some mail to get out and some shopping to do. Why don't you come with me?"

Frederick and I had worked on prairie chickens for years. The whole town knew it, and I knew the local people's stock question.

Kramer and I drove to town.

The postmaster smiled and asked, "How are the chickens?" I smiled knowingly at Kramer.

The grocer just asked me what I wanted, but a dear old man wearing an ancient red plaid jacket and a toothless smile wandered over to me and asked, "How are the chickens?"

That did it. Kramer was convinced.

It is my misfortune that I never had the chance to watch him walk up to a total stranger in the United States of America and ask with charm and confidence, "How are the chickens?"

But Kramer's troubles weren't over, nor were mine.

The gabboons—to show what dainty table manners they had—stuck out their little fingers at mealtimes. Some of them, only fairly surreptitiously, opened their flannel shirts, exposing great hairy chests, or pulled up their sweaters, exposing their stomachs, to let me know that they were *not* wearing undershirts. Jack and maybe two others tried to prevent this display.

The gabboons were taking sides! But mercifully, no fight broke out in front of Kramer.

Sometimes it was just me against the gabboons. For weeks they had used an irritating expression. Over and over again when Frederick or I had asked a difficult question the reply had been, "I just don't know *what* to say." And each and every one simpered when he said it. It was maddening.

I had taken a good deal of satisfaction by walking up to any gabboon who came out with this idiot phrase, looking him straight in the eye, and saying, "Ich weiss nicht wo ich spucken soll."

None of them knew German and none had the faintest idea that what I really said at them in disgust was, "I just don't know where to spit."

Jack had a good deal of control over the gabboons and this time he was on my side. Never once did he expose his hairy chest at mealtimes, and I don't think he once raised his little finger to advertise how dearie-delicate his table manners were supposed to be. Jack not only was Senior Gabboon but he had memorized that one German phrase. He happened to be leaning against the music room door when Kramer asked him a question that he couldn't answer. He straightened up, and his answer was like a field of daisies in June—so sure, so right. Jack answered, ''Ich weiss nicht wo ich spucken soll.''

His accent was perfect.

Grand Central West

Once the word was out that prairie chicken watching was both adventurous and useful, we soon had to turn away up to 140 applicants each year.

Evening after evening as new groups arrived we hoped they would be on time. Some students had been coached in an almost military manner: they formed a line with their sleeping bags over their shoulders and waited, almost at attention, to be shown their sleeping quarters. Our house was built by an English gentleman named Walker, the first judge of Waushara County. It has high ceilings, transoms over the doors, and although we have lived in it since 1949, I still don't know how many rooms it has. Most of the boomers slept in the ballroom—an upstairs ballroom that runs the full length of the house. It holds five double-decker cots and sometimes three single cots as well. These take up much of the floor space; the walls are lined with dress forms, costume trunks, deer antlers, two antiquated sewing machines, books, tennis racquets, and more. . . . Cobwebs form interesting patterns on the unplastered walls, bats squeak in the rafters, and squirrels scuttle in the walls.

Our ballroom appears untidy, but it is full of items we might have use for some day. We kept the guest rooms tidy and reserved them for couples. We have four guest rooms with double beds and an extra nook with a double bed in one of the upstairs halls. All in all we could sleep twenty-three people without dislodging a member of the family. Twenty-three was far too many to help with the chickens at one time, and we tried to hold the numbers of boomers down to about half the capacity of the house.

Our children grew up with the booming season as a natural part of spring. Sometimes they mingled with the boomers, and sometimes they didn't even look up from their books or toys. (Most American adults don't notice children anyway.) Each evening they watched a dozen or so ornithologists, hunters, students, Europeans, New Zealanders, South Americans, grouse experts, etc., come through the kitchen and go upstairs lugging their duffle.

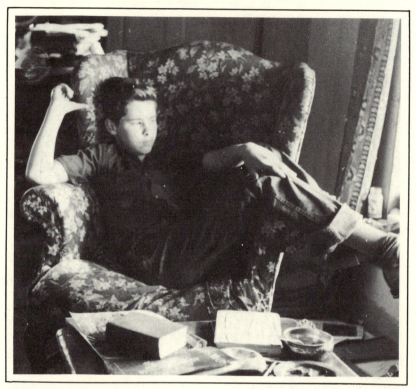

ALAN, OBLIVIOUS OF BOOMERS, MUSES

One late afternoon our car got stuck on the marsh and we finally got home about nine-thirty—two hours after the boomers had arrived. Elva—about eleven at the time—met us at the door. "I showed them their beds, and I briefed them because you didn't come."

Frederick and I were both exhausted. He said, "Good evening," to the mass of assembled men standing in our living room. He took a deep breath and started firing questions at one and then another:

"How do you distinguish between a cock and a hen?"

"The cocks have three-inch neck tufts. Hens have one-inch tufts. If it booms, it's a cock."

"When are you to map the territories?"

"When there are no hens on the booming ground."
"How do you know if a copulation is successful?"
"The hen ruffles her feathers all up, the cock chases another cock, and the hen leaves the grounds inside of five to ten minutes."

One after another the answers came back, prompt and correct.

Frederick got out the jug of red wine. "The briefing is over. Now I'll assign you to blinds."

I started cooking breakfast for sixteen. Whoever didn't give the briefing got breakfast started. Count out 16 plates; put 32 eggs in a bowl; fry 16 slices of bacon till almost done; make a big pot of coffee. Elva joined me in the kitchen. "Perhaps you could let Hammy know that the man with the Badger T-shirt is color-blind: he can't go alone."

I slipped Frederick the message and congratulated our small daughter for having done a fine job.

It never seemed quite polite to write total strangers and say, "Come at 7:30 P.M., *but don't come before.*" As a result a good many groups of boomers arrived before. They arrived before we had finished eating our supper, or even earlier. This was fine if they were old friends, but it was awkward to cook, eat, plan the work, and entertain new arrivals simultaneously. Frederick just moaned when carloads arrived early: we needed one reasonably quiet meal. He prefers a rather hermit-like existence anyway; he likes to plan ahead, and when Alan suddenly named our ancient farmhouse *Grand Central West* at supper one evening, Frederick sputtered, "That's just what it is!" I had just ladled the stew into bowls, when car doors slammed in the driveway. "Damn it," he continued, "I haven't even read day before yesterday's mail and here come the smiling faces."

I rushed outside to intercept the group and returned in a moment or two. "They'll be back at exactly 7:30."

"Who were they?"

"I haven't any idea. They're boomers. Darling, I *did* read day before yesterday's mail: the state wants us to band woodcock, and those people are out there right now pinpointing the peenting grounds for us. I told them how to listen for male woodcock making the peenting noise. They find the peenting grounds; we trap the woodcock."

We had our supper in peace.

Soon the woodcock project became so fascinating that we began to welcome early boomers. The minute I detected their arrival, I intercepted them, handed them some pieces of paper towel, and asked them to mark each peenting ground as exactly as possible. The next evening we set our vertical, almost invisible mist nets by the markers and made our catch. This fine symbiotic relationship didn't always go smoothly. A group of wildlife students from Minnesota marked more peenting grounds than any other group. Rain kept us from setting up the nets but didn't keep me from sending the next bunch of early birds out to listen for woodcock . . . just to listen . . . that's all I asked them to do.

At 7:30 the group reappeared. The leader, a young man, radiated a noble glow and his group stood behind him beaming. "We found a lot of litter and picked it up." He and the members of his party held out pieces of paper towel as though they had just accomplished some fantastic ceremony.

"Put them back," I roared. "Those are markers. Do you know how to put them back?"

"No," he gasped.

He took the markers from each member of his party and headed for the wastepaper basket.

"Don't throw them away. They'll all go out again tomorrow night if we're lucky enough to have a good crew."

I took the towel scraps from him and put them in a paper bag. "You couldn't help it," I said kindly. Apparently not a single member of that group noticed that each piece of towelling had been fastened to the ground with a stick and that by some astounding coincidence peenting woodcock had led them unerringly to their precious "litter!"

Frederick asked me, "Would you like to give the briefing tonight?"

My answer was short. "Not at all."

I went out and netted a couple of woodcock. This put me in a better frame of mind, but we had lost our big catch that spring.

Look out for the English

We were pretty well tuckered out, for the home crew had been out well before daylight for seven weeks. We didn't just get up early once or twice; we did it every day, seven days a week. And the day hadn't started out just right—nothing really wrong. One lady, the last to come downstairs for breakfast, arranged a whole row of bottles, jars, skin creams and such on the wash bench in the kitchen. Quick eaters had almost finished their scrambled eggs, and the slow eaters were making good progress. Frederick left the table to see why there was still an untouched plate. He viewed the array on the wash bench in horror. The lady smiled and said, "I'm going to wash my face," and added, unscrewing the cap of a bulbous pink jar, "I do this every morning."

Frederick moved closer, almost blocking her from some of her equipment. "You will either wash your face or you will eat breakfast."

The lady raised silent pleading eyes, like a begging puppy and gave a little sob, pushed her possessions into some sort of a rubberized sponge bag, and rushed toward the only plate of bacon and eggs.

Dick Hunt announced, "Let's get going. The North End is about to leave. Line your cars up back of mine."

The lady redoubled her efforts with her fork, but found Frederick looking at her. She reached for a paper napkin and whispered, "I can just take this with me."

"No food in the blinds!" he ordered.

I slid in beside her, "Look, just eat, don't argue."

I tried to find her later to explain why we can't let people take food into the blinds. They leave waxed paper, banana peels, and all sorts of stuff that we have to clean up later.

A BOOMER EMERGES

Toward the end of the booming season we got a frost warning. A frost warning in mid-May puts us all on edge: it means that hens are apt to return to the booming grounds in substantial numbers. We need a fine group of observers to cope with reading band numbers in spite of rather tall grass, and we want excellent notes. Frederick said, "What sort of people are we having tonight?"

I got up from the supper table and handed him the list. "That boy, Kozlovsky, was here before and did a good job, Mike Cudahay brought us a whole side of bacon last year, but I don't remember what his notes were like; I think all the others are new. Mr. and Mrs. English were highly recommended and they are bringing *two* scopes."

The boomers came piling in just as we finished supper. I showed them their beds, welcomed them, and gave them routine instructions like, "Wear your boots to breakfast. We leave immediately afterwards, and nobody has a chance to run upstairs to get anything he might have forgotten."

Frederick started making preliminary lists of who had hip boots, who had brought his own scope, who wanted to photograph, etc. "Where are Mr. and Mrs. English?"

"I'm putting them in Posey's room; they aren't here yet."

7:40. "Have the English come yet?"

"No."

8:17. "Fran, will you read that letter from the English and make sure they have the right date?"

I handed Frederick the letter. They had the right date.

9:04. Frederick herded everybody into the big room. We had waited long enough for the English. In fact, we had never delayed starting the briefing so long before.

At 7:15 that same evening our good neighbors, Mr. and Mrs. Crawford, watched a strange car turn into their driveway; a moment later, a young couple bounded into their house and shook hands. "We're the English."

Mrs. English stooped swiftly and exclaimed, "What a darling puppy," while Mr. English seated himself on the sofa.

They admired the lovely old farmhouse, the Wisconsin countryside, and the ladies shared an interest in home upholstery. I suppose the conversation may have flagged a little from time to time, for the English—patiently waiting for the briefing to start—failed to state their business. Country courtesy kept the Crawfords from asking the direct question: Why are you here? And unexpected visitors were such a rare treat that it was not until 10:00, almost three hours after the unexpected guests had arrived, that Mrs. Crawford brought out coffee and cake: the country signal that it's time for guests to go home.

Mr. and Mrs. English enjoyed the cake and coffee and settled themselves even more comfortably on the Crawford sofa.

After a while Mr. English inquired, "When are the Hamerstroms coming?"

"The *Hamerstroms?* Why we don't expect the Hamerstroms tonight."

Mr. English leapt to his feet. "You mean they don't *live* here?"

"Why, no," Mrs. Crawford said gently, "they live way over there. We can sometimes see their lights from here. They must have gone to bed. They have to get up terribly early every morning . . . long before daybreak."

The Hamerstroms had finally gone to bed. And after a brief, peaceful sleep, there was a scratching sound on the windowsill. Frederick turned his head slowly and saw a man trying to help a woman through our bedroom window.

I was awakened by the roar of my man: "What the Hell do you think you are doing?"

Frederick always puts on his slippers and bathrobe before emerging. Barefoot, in his pajamas, I rushed outdoors. My flashlight found them right by our window. "Who are you?"

"We're the English. We didn't want to disturb you."

"Then why didn't you walk in a door? They're unlocked."

"Unlocked?"

"Did you really bring two scopes?

"I'll show you to your room. We'll call you at two. That's in about three hours. Sleep quick."

The next morning Frederick said, "I'd have killed them if I'd had a baseball bat." It was a bad beginning, but we learned to love the English.

Raincoat

From time to time all Pittman-Robertson projects are subject to federal inspection. Inspectors traveled in pairs and always announced when they were coming. On August 15, 1959, they were coming to review our project.

We never dreaded these visitations; the inspectors were biologists, and we looked forward to the chance to discuss our project. I straightened the house up a bit, made sure that I had plenty of good food on hand and, as the inspectors were not due until 9 o'clock, I went kestrel trapping. It seemed a pity to waste a day, as these little hawks were passing through on migration in goodly numbers.

I just thought I'd run up and down the road to see if I couldn't catch one or two before the inspectors arrived.

Trapping was fabulous. I set two small balchatris—little cages baited with mice—by the roadside and caught two birds before I could get the car turned around. Then I noticed that while I had been cleaning up the house, Frederick had been cleaning up the car: my bands, tubes, and scales were all back at the house.

I put one kestrel in my purse, leaving the top slightly open, and looked around for something to put the next one into. (Frederick had been thorough.) All I could find was my raincoat and I feared the kestrel might smother in that, so I took off my shoes and socks and put the bird in a sock. By then I had caught *three* more birds! I slipped one of these into the other sock and then—holding two kestrels in one hand—I put on the raincoat, took off my slacks, and fastened the remaining two birds into the pants legs.

The sun was getting fairly high and the heat was beginning to beat down. Common sense should have suggested that it was time to quit and go home, but I never gave it a thought. Another kestrel was working one of the traps, and there were two more sitting on a wire just down the road. I baited and set out another balchatri and caught three more. I muttered "Damn female clothes." *My* slacks had no pockets—but my shirt did.

123

Looking carefully up and down the road to make sure no one was in sight, I took off the raincoat, took off my shirt, and hastily donned the raincoat again. It was all I had on.

A kestrel apiece went into each pocket of my shirt, and I tied one into a sleeve.

So far there had been no traffic. A farm truck went by and brought me to my senses. It was so hot that the birds in their unusual containers might suffer heat stroke. Thank heavens I hadn't put any bird in a raincoat sleeve; the broiling sun made this long, impermeable garment almost unbearable. I drove home quickly.

There was a strange car in the driveway—a long, low car bearing the unmistakable insignia of the United States on its well-polished door. I had forgotten the inspection.

I considered climbing in the window of our bedroom to change clothes, but the window was closed against the heat and our old-fashioned windows couldn't be pried open. Frederick and the inspectors were sitting at the living room table, and there was only one way to get to my clothes; I rushed past them in my long, floppy raincoat and slammed the bedroom door.

A few minutes later I emerged smiling and bombarded the inspectors with questions about prairie chickens to keep them from asking me what I'd been up to. I wasn't paid to work on hawks and, although in those far-gone days a "biologist's time was his own," I didn't want to explain why I was rushing about in the sunlight in a raincoat.

It took me a little longer than usual to prepare lunch that day because I was banding and processing kestrels in the kitchen at the same time.

After the inspectors left, Frederick asked, "What on earth were you doing in that raincoat?"

He was not prepared for my rejoinder. "Oh, darling, do you think they noticed?"

124

Halloween

When our children were small, we received a perfectly standard invitation (printed) to attend the annual meeting of the German Ornithological Society, which I had joined because they sometimes had good papers on grouse in their journal—and prairie chickens are grouse too.

I rushed to Frederick and shouted, "Look! We're invited to a meeting in Germany." Our son, age seven, and our daughter, age five, followed me into the study, noticing that something beyond the normal excitement of the household was up.

Frederick looked at the "invitation" with mild interest. "Just think!" I shouted, "we can study black cock and capercaillie. They are so closely related to prairie chickens. It is our *duty* to accept."

He looked again at the piece of paper. No expenses; just printed; nothing personal; and then he gave me his answer. "It's impossible. We can't do it. We don't have the money."

For three or four days I burned most of the meals—not on purpose—and I walked in the woods to soothe my soul—and I wrote poetry. I think I managed to get the whole darn thing out of my system in five days. Hopeless, we can't go.

Then I forgot it.

About two weeks later Frederick asked, "Where would we leave the children?"

"Leave the children? *When?*"

"Leave the children *if* we go to Europe."

"No problem. There's my mother, and Aunt Ethel. And lots of people love our children. It is very bad for children just to be brought up by their parents. They should be exposed to numerous good adults."

Before we could study grouse in the marshes, moors, and mountains of Bavaria, other arrangements had to be made. After we arrived in Germany, Adalbert Ebner, of the German Forest Service,

125

spent a number of days telephoning, coaxing, and trying to line up the right contacts for us. At last he announced, "We are in—totally in. Oberforstmeister Karl Beringer, the chief forester, has personally invited us to afternoon coffee."

Adalbert looked at us appraisingly, "You will make a very good impression." He said it again, as though to convince himself. "A very good impression." Americans were not particularly popular right after Germany had lost a war. Plainly, Adalbert wanted to tell me not to wear the tattered jeans that I persisted in wearing in the woods.

The next day we took the train for Marquartstein where a junior forester was to meet us. Adalbert relaxed when we got on the train. He said, "Fran, you always do things perfectly—just right for the occasion—it is an art."

I was wearing a plain white peasant blouse, a handwoven Bavarian skirt, and only another woman would have detected that I was wearing any makeup at all.

Both men were wearing those little green hats with chamois beards sticking up at the sides. We got happily off the train and started to wait. I jumped up onto a luggage truck, swung my legs, and admired the scenery while the men paced up and down the railroad platform. Everybody is always a little late in Bavaria, so it took us quite a while to realize that nobody was coming to meet us. Something had gone wrong.

Adalbert asked for directions, and we trudged up steep mountainous roads to our destination. Beringer, bowing, met us at the door. He exclaimed in distress, "But you walked!" We pointed out that we were sorry to be late but no one had met us.

Beringer jumped to the telephone and ordered, "Schuster is to appear immediately." And in a very few minutes a tall blond forester arrived.

Beringer looked at him scathingly. "Didn't I tell you to meet the Americans on the three o'clock train?"

"Yes, sir."

"And why didn't you?"

"There were no Americans on the train."

Schuster got a good dressing down. He kept peeking at me. There was no way he could explain that he thought all American women wore horrid bright colors and too much makeup, and it wasn't until I spoke to Frederick in English that he really believed that the girl he'd seen sitting on the baggage truck was actually American.

126

The house of the chief forester was almost royal. Persian rugs lay on polished floors, brocade drapes graced tall windows, and heavy, spookily carved dark furniture looked as though it had been in the family since the Middle Ages. Frau Beringer—a magnificent brunette—poured coffee into delicate china cups and two beautiful teenage daughters passed cakes on silver platters.

Herr Beringer was the most magnificent sight of all. He stood a bit over six feet, with his curly gray hair in the first Einstein haircut I'd ever seen (the year was 1949). Dark eyes flashed dangerously under fine black brows, and his arching nostrils made him look like a proud prince out of some ancient fairy tale. Seldom—if ever—have I beheld a man with such an aristocratic and haughty bearing.

After coffee Herr Beringer invited Frederick to look at his gun collection. I followed close at their heels, but Frau Beringer pulled me gently away. "Let's let the men talk."

I couldn't tell her that I didn't want to miss a single one of her husband's hunting stories, so I followed her. She showed me the house, which struck me as a cross between a castle and a museum. Dazed by the splendor and beauty, I didn't know what to expect when she said, "Would you like to have me show you something special?"

I nodded, and was guided to the kitchen. Frau Beringer linked her arm with mine and stood perfectly still. Plainly there was something I was supposed to admire, but I hadn't the foggiest notion what it might be. Overwhelmed by the fantastic things I'd seen in the last hour, I was at a loss.

She gave my arm a little squeeze, disengaged it, and opened the refrigerator door. "Think of it. It is an electric American refrigerator!" It was touching. She and her daughters dusted and polished and cared for the treasures of the ages in that huge house. They did it with love and understanding, and now their work would be a little lighter.

Herr Beringer took us to the railroad station in his car when our research came to a close. And then he stood on the railroad platform and waved and waved again with a large white handkerchief. And we waved back. Paths sometimes cross for so short a time.

But the train didn't leave the station. We waved and he waved. Minutes seemed to turn into hours. Here was Oberforstmeister Karl Beringer waving a handkerchief at us, and we were getting to feel more and more foolish waving back. He waved with perfect aplomb, and plainly planned to keep waving until we were out of sight.

At last we left our seats and went to the open door. Just then the train gave a lurch and got under way. I shouted, "You must come to see *us* sometime."

We watched Beringer getting smaller and smaller in the distance till we could barely see him waving his handkerchief. Heavens only knew when we'd ever get to Europe again. He'd probably be dead.

Back in Wisconsin we returned to our rigorous routine and published a paper on our European findings as well. An airmail letter from Germany arrived in August. I struggled through the miserable handwriting and announced, "Beringer is coming."

Frederick—considerably startled—asked, *"Here?"*

"It's all right. I'll warn him."

I wrote Beringer airmail, an honest—and maybe even lurid—account of our circumstances. "We do not live the way you do. We live in an ancient farmhouse without plumbing. We pump our own water, and the house, built before the Civil War, is crumbling apart—no telling when a ceiling is going to fall down. Of course you're very welcome, but I thought we'd better let you know. We do have good hunting."

Beringer replied, "I can only stay with you a week."

A *week!* We planned that week. Forestry tours, grouse hunting, and we planned every single evening so he could savor something new in the United States.

After he arrived, we planned to introduce Oberforstmeister Karl Beringer to American Negro spirituals. Anybody with all that culture had better hear them. It happened to be Halloween night.

Our children, Alan and Elva, got dressed up and appeared in our living room. "Excuse me for a few minutes. It's Halloween. I'm taking the children to town and I'll be right back."

"Is this Halloween a National Festival?"

"I don't really think so. . . . We have some fantastic music—American spirituals—that we are sure you want to hear."

I took Alan and Elva dressed up as ghosts to Plainfield and rushed back to entertain our distinguished guest. Frederick had produced a bottle of red wine and was preparing the record player.

Beringer met me at the door. "How often does this not quite National Festival occur?"

Finally, I caught on. "Would you *rather* go to Plainfield?"

"Yess. That would be preferable to me."

Frederick stashed away the records, and we set off for town: Honor Bright, with no plan in mind.

128

As we moved past the Johnsons' house I asked Frederick to stop. "Stop *here*."

Quickly, in German, I briefed Herr Oberforstmeister Karl Beringer. "Walk up to that door, ring the bell, and demand, "Trick or treat."

Dear old Mrs. Johnson opened the door expecting small children. She found herself confronted, not by little children, but by a tall, terrifying man whose black eyes and arched nostrils loomed in the half-light. Beringer took one step toward her, bowed, and bellowed, "Trrrick or trreet!"

Mrs. Johnson gasped, held her hand to her mouth to stifle a scream, and clutched the door frame.

Frederick and I were hiding behind some spirea bushes to watch the fun. But Frederick decided the fun had gone a little too far so he leapt to the porch to reassure her. She had known him at least twenty years, but now she failed to recognize him. Two giant men confronted her at her own door: trick or treating!

Fortunately, Elisabeth Johnson appeared at that moment. "It's all right, Mother. It's just the Hamerstroms."

But even Miss Johnson, who had been a major in the United States Army and had traveled over much of the world, looked a bit startled when Beringer towered over her and bowed.

Competing foundations

Very few people like tongue. My parents often served cold cuts for summer luncheons and then the children got cold tongue for supper for several days thereafter. I find cold tongue with a dab of sharp mustard absolutely delicious.

When it came time to do something for the chickens, to save them before their range disappeared, Frederick and I gave a series of luncheons on the lawn under the elms. We invited influential conservationists, to try to stir up interest in saving a species that many thought was already doomed in Wisconsin. We hoarded our money for these occasions and bought ham, cheese, tongue, sandwich bread, and, of course beer. And we expounded on the plight of the chickens.

Without exception these luncheons all ended in the same way. Everyone agreed that "something must be done for the chickens." Then they all got back into their Cadillacs and drove away. The only tangible result of these parties was that the Hamerstroms had enough leftover tongue for dinner—for supper—for breakfast.

But over 7,000 people came to watch the prairie chickens booming and the chickens themselves produced one dark horse and then another.

An old hunter spoke up at the Second Breakfast one day. "You know, I'm a member of the Wisconsin Conservation League. We're all getting old and were just planning to disband. We have some money left in the kitty."

Money!

The League was delighted to buy eighty acres of chicken land with the money in the kitty.

The next dark horse was Paul Olson of the Dane County Conservation League. He watched the prairie chickens boom on the Buena Vista Marsh and promptly launched the Prairie Chicken Foundation.

PAUL OLSON

I quote: "Let the boys at Canaveral hurl their rockets at the moon and at whatever swirling worlds there are. I respect their discipline and their sense of high adventure—but in the cold predawn of the Buena Vista as I listen to one of the last authentic truly wild American voices—I achieve *my* adventure."

The Prairie Chicken Foundation (with the help of a dark horse of its own) bought many acres of chicken land.

Then, too, there were private purchases by individuals. The Gordon Kummers made the first. Reuben and Meta Paulson, farmers from the southern part of the state said, "I guess we can make our old car do another year." They bought eighty acres. And so did the Clarence Jungs—right where the domain of the chickens was about to be threatened by agro-industry.

Dory Kummer Vallier has a knack for running into just the right people at just the right time. She ran into Bill Sullivan and said, "Bill, you've just got to help the prairie chicken."

"HELP THE PRAIRIE CHICKEN? HELL, I DIDN'T KNOW HE WAS IN TROUBLE."
—*Bill Sullivan*

131

It was so that the Society of Tympanuchus Cupido Pinnatus was formed. Bill elected himself "Tympanuchus," Jack Pelisek became the "Quill" (Secretary) and Bill selected a "Council of Chiefs."

Frederick and I watched this amazing organization grow. He opined, "Good works do not have to be done in a sepulchral atmosphere."

A GATHERING OF PRAIRIE CHICKEN ENTHUSIASTS, AS DEPICTED IN *BOOM*, THE STCP NEWSLETTER. . .

The Society's address is: S.T.C.P., John Best, Secretary, 250 E. Wisconsin Ave., Milwaukee, WI 53202. (Not everybody can get in, but it's worth a try.)

Luncheon parties under the elms and leftover tongue now seem long, long ago. Two foundations lease lands to the Wisconsin Department of Natural Resources and amicably compete with each other to save the chickens. Now each spring the prairie chickens boom and the mellow sound rolls over the meadows. They are doing well, but more land set aside would make it even more likely that Wisconsin will keep its chickens forever.

132

Easy! Take one of each! (Bill Sullivan Jr., Bill Van Dyke III)

Oh, it'll come out right . . . (Walter Malzahn, T. W. Tuttle)

I like shrimp, but the sauce gets me right here (Jacque Vallier, George Kasten)

I know what I'm going to take . . (Charles Pain)

You timing it? (Eliot Fitch, Jim Windham)

Take shrimp and 7 points? (Fred Hamerstrom, Dick Herzfeld)

DECISIONS! DECISIONS! SHRIMP — OR CREAM CHEESE WITH OLIVE?

Lost in study over the hors d'oeuvre tray at the annual meeting were Gordon Black, Bob Trainer and Grigsby Markham. Their agonizing moment of truth didn't really draw all the attention you might think from its treatment on this page — but wouldn't it have been fun if it had?

No! No! Not the shrimp! (Bill Lent, Nelson Ross)

That's how crackers crumble . . (Charles Nelson, Bill Sullivan)

Shrimp!   Cream cheese! (John Burke, Dick Fisher, Clarence Jung)

It's the suspense that's unbearable . . .

With me, it's barbecued beef Steve Borhegyi)

Going into Society

Smokey the Bear has perhaps been the worst enemy of the prairie chicken. They thrive after a fire! John Curtis, the great ecologist, stated that in Wisconsin the white man has changed the north by fire protection even more than he has changed the south by intensive agriculture.

Frederick calls Smokey the Bear the greatest ecological hoax ever perpetrated on an unsuspecting public.

Fire is a natural and a necessary part of our landscape. John Curtis has *set* fires to save orchids. Game managers are now setting fires (known as controlled burns) to save prairie chickens. Prairie orchids and prairie chickens alike face extirpation when vegetation gets too tall.

Not all fires are good. Some do enormous damage. And controlled burns must be set not only in the right place but also at the right time of year. That day—so long ago—when I played tennis and failed to fight fire is a good case in point. A fire, catastrophic because it swept over the Great Plain during the nesting season, sealed the doom of a whole race. But fire was nevertheless essential to the survival of the heath hen. Now we know that controlled burns at the right time of year might have saved that bird from extinction.

The Great Plain was roughly the size of our study area, and our study area had one of the densest prairie chicken populations in the world.

In 1941 there were prairie chickens in every county in Wisconsin, including Milwaukee County with all its cities and subdivisions. But those nice, untidy farms in the northern part of the state were obliterated by *zoning:* people were moved out and the forest took over. And in the southern counties intensive agriculture, perhaps combined with competition from the Chinese ring-necked pheasant, obliterated flock after flock.

The decline of the heath hen and of the prairie chicken was

LET HER ROAR—SAVING A PRAIRIE   *(Betsy Doehlert)*

variously blamed on disease, on overhunting, on foxes, on cats abandoned by the summer people and left to go wild, and on "them white owls."

We drew blood from prairie chickens and examined the guts of shot birds to test for disease. We were able to rule out overhunting. The decline of the prairie chicken was plainly not due to cats, foxes, or owls. It was like a jigsaw puzzle with one of the pieces missing, and at last we found the missing piece. Prairie chickens needed a *home*. The hens needed the right sort of place to lay their eggs and rear their young. This wasn't their only requirement. It was just the hardest piece to fit into the puzzle.

Somehow we had sense enough not to stop after our great discovery. (Habitat is a household world now, but it wasn't then.) Frederick was offered chances to triple his salary if he'd go to Washington. (He just laughed.) Now that we had found a key to part of the puzzle, we had a lot to find out. The foundations were buying

135

land in forty-acre blocks. How far apart should these purchases be? Only banded birds could tell us.

We named each purchase and one of these, bought by the Society of Tympanuchus Cupido Pinnatus, soon just became "Society." It was a fine piece of nest-brood cover, and a food patch on it turned out to be a good trapping station in winter. It was on my trapline.

Late winter is a particularly good time to catch prairie chickens. They are down in weight and push eagerly toward the bait. My trapline consisted of twenty-seven miles and I had a lot of ground to cover. I took a shortcut and rammed the car into a major snowdrift. It can't have taken me much more than an hour to shovel out, back up about half a mile and go around the long way; but I had a good catch, and it took me some time to process all the birds.

One more station to run! And I was about two hours behind schedule already! I'll never know what caused my next mishap, but the car slithered off the road. Now I not only had to shovel but I had to jack up the rear wheels and put boards under them to get moving again.

It was Sunday, and the road into Society was terrible. Actually I hadn't expected to get stuck until I hit that road. The Wagon Wheel Tavern was on the way to Society, and they had a telephone. The barkeep was busy. Church was over and the tavern was jammed. There were no women in the tavern, and my arrival aroused a certain amount of attention. An amiable drunk asked me what I would have, and gradually conversation practically ceased while everybody watched developments, as in desperation I explained I didn't want a drink. I wanted to telephone. A man in overalls on a nearby barstool nodded toward the telephone. It was behind the bar, well out of reach of the customers.

I jumped, threw my belly on the bar, reached across, and seized the phone. By now everybody was listening. I called home and, worried lest I not be able to reach the birds in the traps in time, I must have sounded utterly distraught. "I'm going into Society and if I'm not back in an hour rescue me."

I rushed out of the tavern, jumped into my car, and disappeared. I can almost imagine those in the tavern, "Know what that woman said? I heard her."

"Yeah, I heard her too."

And he played the electric guitar

One of the biggest landowners in the prairie chicken country was something of a mystery man. He posted his vast acreage with conspicuous signs—TRESPASSERS WILL BE PROSECUTED—and was occasionally seen to patrol the edges of his domain in a big black Cadillac. He may have spoken to me once when I was trapping a broad-winged hawk that I wanted to band. At any rate the big black car slid up beside mine, and a man with a strong Chicago accent wanted to know what I was doing. There were prairie chickens on his land; he was reputed to be rich, and if I hadn't been so startled I would have tried to persuade him to set aside portions of his land for prairie chickens to nest on—instead of plowing up almost all of his property.

His dark glasses masked his facial expression. His voice was unfriendly, so that I didn't even pull myself together enough to ask permission to go on his land to count the booming prairie cocks in spring.

We needed those counts.

I took matters into my own hands the following spring. I pulled on hip boots, and very early one morning I drove straight onto The Big D Ranch, sneaking in on an almost unused farm trail. I hoped to get the chickens counted and be gone before anybody was up and about.

The road was unused for good reason. When I had barely made it through puddles for not quite a mile, the bottom dropped out of the road and I sank my truck in mud—down to all four hubcaps. Time to face the music. I had to go to those Chicago-type farm buildings and ask somebody to get out a tractor. I brushed my hair, and when I got quite close to the buildings, I took off my jacket and hung it over my arm to hide its raggedness. Men are usually gentler with a woman, and I was glad that I, not Frederick, had to confess trespass!

I didn't enjoy walking up to the front door of that big, modernized farmhouse. And I felt even more uneasy when a handsome, swarthy man with curly black hair said, "Step right in." But the voice was mellower than the one I remembered.

"I've done something awful. I got my truck stuck about half a mile north of here."

"Yeah?"

"I'm stuck on your property and it's going to take a tractor to get it out."

"I'll send out the boys."

"Oh," I exclaimed quickly, "I'll go out with them and help."

"It's breakfast time. You stay and have breakfast with me." This man didn't sound unfriendly at all. "Annie," he called into the kitchen, "fix breakfast for two, and make some of them muffins."

"Ever hear an electric guitar?" Without waiting for an answer he took a guitar out of its case, seated himself on the sofa next to me, and started playing *Santa Lucia.* The delicate aroma of bacon floated into the living room. I studied my host's face. It was a strong face, but it didn't look mean.

He looked at me inquiringly after he finished, and I said, "That was lovely, Mr. . . ?"

"Just call me Sid."

"Yes, Sid."

He played another tune and started singing with a good deal of gusto and rolling out his *r*'s like an Italian opera singer. The music was awfully loud, and I was glad when Annie came in to set the table. I knew Annie! She was one of our neighbors! I said hello, but Annie just barely nodded her head and kept right on putting breakfast on the table.

My chance had come! I let Sid eat a few mouthfuls to put him in a good mood, and then I told him about the prairie chickens on his own property and how wonderful it would be if he would set some land aside and just keep it in grass.

"You want me to do that?" he asked.

"*Could* you?"

"How much land do ya want in grass?"

"Well, the best would be about forty acres in each square mile."

Sid swallowed the last mouthful of his breakfast, pushed his plate back and said, "That's only about one sixteenth of the ranch . . . not much of a problem."

I could hardly wait to get home to tell Frederick, and the boys had just returned with my truck. Annie's husband was one of "the boys."

138

"Got another song you might like to hear." Sid took up the guitar again, and I didn't dare offend him by telling him I was supposed to be at home cooking for a houseful of boomers and helping Frederick check their notes.

Sid knew a lot of songs, but I finally made my escape. It was almost noon by the time I got home. The boomers were gone, and Frederick was washing the dishes by himself. I grabbed a dish towel.

"What happened?" he asked. "Get stuck?"

"Yes, and it was the best thing that ever happened. Darling, the Big D Ranch people are just wonderful. I met the owner and he promised to set aside scattered forties for the chickens. He says it's no problem! No problem at all. He wants to help the prairie chickens. He's perfectly charming."

I looked at the map of the Big D before I went to bed and dreamed of flocks of chickens and the sound of their melodious booming all over the ranch in spring.

A few days later I ran into Annie in the post office. "Annie! What a wonderful man you work for!"

"Huh?"

"Sid—he's going to change the farm plan and set lots of land aside for the chickens."

Annie wrinkled her nose. "That Sid ain't the owner. He's hired help just like me—and he got fired yesterday."

Of possums and public relations

Anybody who is in danger of becoming a living myth had better proceed with caution. Some people have an absolute knack for getting talked about; it is one of my failings, and not all the talk helped the Prairie Chicken Project.

I've found the myths to be based on fact, and when you get down to the kernel of truth in the story, it is based on an innocent episode . . . for which nobody had requested an explanation.

For example, we had two tame horned owls on our front porch, Ambrose and Zuleika, and we hoped that they would breed there. Wild horned owls came to visit our tame owls and sat in the tall elms in front of the house and made music in the evenings. I wanted the wild owls nearer so I could watch them better, so I devised a "visiting owl's chair."

One Sunday morning in spring, when the frost was out of the ground, the neighbors passing our house on the way to church saw me and my son Alan digging a big hole in the front lawn. I can almost hear their comments: "Isn't it nice? Maybe Mrs. Hamerstrom is going to put in a rosebush."

Alan and I worked fast, and on their way back from church the neighbors were treated to the sight of two people planting the grayish, knobby trunk of a long-dead tree. Nobody stopped to ask why we planted a dead tree, but some of the neighbors tended to be a bit self-conscious when returning my friendly waves.

This wasn't so bad because what I was doing out by the front door was not being paid for with taxpayers' money. I tried hard to conform, and I don't think it was until August that I *perfectly innocently* gave somebody another story to spread.

There was a banded male marsh hawk that I passionately wanted to catch. He ignored all the usual traps, so I fashioned a series of small nooses and put them on his favorite fence post, hoping to catch him by his toes. I hid and watched that bird. He chose a new post. I

140

moved the contraption to his new post and he selected another. The only thing to do was to shag him back to his old favorite perch by making all the other potential perches unattractive to him.

I got up early the next morning, armed with 100 rubber bands and a large kitchen knife. I cut vegetation and fastened each bunch to a fence post, leaving only his favorite post with nothing on it but that little circle of nooses.

At last there was no place for him to perch but on that one post. I looked around. There was a pickup parked by the road, and somebody had been watching me for heaven only knows how long. Then I looked around again. The goldenrod was in full bloom and had been by far the easiest vegetation to cut. I had decorated almost 100 fence posts with bunches of flowers!

I ran toward the truck, plunging through goldenrod, nettles, and spirea. I waved and called to the man in the truck. I *had* to catch him and explain what I was doing and why, but he drove away. This was more serious: I was out on the study area, and I felt another myth on its way to that mysterious country telegraph that passes on juicy morsels of information: "Know what us taxpayers are paying for now? Those prairie chicken people are putting *flowers* on top of fence posts! Flowers! And you and I gotta pay for it."

Rumors started sizzling, and more and more fuel was added. During the past winter when the snows had been deep, we had simply unset one prairie chicken trapping station by tipping all the traps upside down so the birds could feed on our bait at will. That story got back to us: ". . . they left them traps out in the field and they never went back. I'd hate to tell you how many chickens froze to death. There wasn't a single snowshoe track into that field for more than two *weeks!*"

When the story got back to us, we explained that the traps had not been set and not a single prairie chicken had died in them, but how many people had heard the story and believed it? Stories have a way of shifting. More than likely this one was what got the next one going: "They are putting so many bands on the legs of those birds that they can't fly."

Frederick, with his gentle politeness, explained to everyone he had a chance to talk with that the three bands we put on each chicken weighed only two grams, and that the chickens weighed about a thousand. Most people had no conception of how heavy a gram might be, so I'd add, "Those bands don't weigh the chickens down any more than a Hershey bar in a man's overcoat pocket weighs him down." Over and over again, we were not believed. We didn't know it then, but things were warming up for what later was to be known as the Prairie Chicken War.

We always tried to do our work well and to be good neighbors too, but now we spent quite a lot of time avoiding criticism.

In late summer the American Ornithologists' Union met in Madison, and after the meeting two carloads of people who wanted to see prairie chickens came home with us. This was unexpected and I didn't have much on hand to feed everybody, so when I saw a lot of fresh ear corn lying by the roadside where a truck had taken a corner too fast, we all got out and picked up corn for supper. Next I stopped for a fresh-dead possum. I find possum too fat to be tasty, but some people like it. Konrad Lorenz, who was in the United States for the first time, eagerly took the possum from me, exclaiming something like "Bauchtier! fabelhaft!" He looked at that possum with as much delight as I would have examined a road-killed kangaroo. Then he left it on his lap and asked questions about the landscape, the animals, the vegetation, and the Indians. It didn't occur to him to ask me about local public relations.

Frederick's carload of ornithologists peppered him with questions, and his car tailed the one I was driving for most of the hundred miles north to our house. But not the very last bit of the way. I turned up the dirt road to our house, and Konrad Lorenz made one of his swift decisions. He glanced to make sure we were being followed. Then he shouted, "Stop!"

I slammed on the brakes.

His reddish beard abristle, and holding the dead possum under his overcoat, he hurled himself into the roadside ditch and pretended to catch a possum. Having "caught" it, he ran up onto the road. Keeping the creature wriggling about in a lifelike manner with his fingers, he pretended to bite it to death. This show was especially for Jean Delacour who was traveling with Frederick.

The car behind us, however, was no longer the one that had followed us from Madison. Two of our most talkative neighbors slowed down and then drove by very slowly. They saw me sitting behind the steering wheel with a frightened expression on my face and watched a huge and ferocious man bite a possum to death in front of their very eyes. Mrs. S. sucked in her lips: she had a story to tell, and as they passed, Mr. S. nodded slowly. He wasn't nodding to me.

The Prairie Chicken War

Frederick can be mighty stubborn. He was asking permission to trap prairie chickens on the land of Mr. L., a local politician, and refused to back down in an argument about foxes and white owls. White owls, which sometimes winter on our marshes, but never in numbers, soon disappeared from the heated discussion. Mrs. L., a broad-shouldered, capable-looking woman, came in to listen and put in her bit about foxes too. "We've got to get rid of the foxes."

Frederick pointed out that there had been foxes and prairie chickens since time immemorial and what we needed was good nest-brood cover. "Look," he said, finally raising his voice. "It doesn't matter how many foxes there are if the chickens have good habitat! What the prairie chickens need is *land,* not fox trappers."

We had crossed swords with an extremely influential man, who happened to make money trapping foxes for bounty, and we had succeeded in irritating him.

Later he and his wife retaliated beyond belief. Mr. L. got "the boys" out and circulated a petition which had hundreds of signatures and was sent to the Governor of Wisconsin. The gist of it was: all you need to do for the prairie chicken is to get rid of the foxes and the Hamerstroms.

We were unaware of the petition being circulated against us, and the first repercussion from the fox discussion came from an unexpected source. Our small son Alan came home from school one afternoon and said to me, "Mrs. L. wants to shoot you."

Neither Frederick nor I laughed. We froze. It was no laughing matter. Alan got himself three peanut butter sandwiches, lay down on the sofa and said, "Don't worry. You're a much better shot than she is."

That petition was the first rumble of the Prairie Chicken War. It was simply filed, but more serious trouble developed some years later. Unbeknownst to us a mass meeting was staged. Frederick

144

walked right into it. One of the game managers appeared at our house and said, "There's going to be a meeting in the town hall tonight. Let's go; they want you to come."

Delighted at a chance to explain the prairie chicken management plan, Frederick, softly humming, rummaged in his study and brought out some maps and charts for his presentation. Then I waved them a cheery good-bye.

To Frederick's astonishment, the town hall was surrounded by cars and more were parked up and down the road. As he approached the building, he could hear the roar of voices like the "zinging" of angry bees in a hive. He walked in. Silence. Suddenly there was absolute silence. Frederick felt a prickle of fear.

Some of the men in the town hall had heard of the management plan and a few had actually seen it.

The plan was for the state to purchase about forty acres per section in a scatter pattern throughout the marsh and keep these areas in good nest-brood cover. We had watched land-use changes and saw the coming need for some land to be managed just for chickens. Frederick showed his map and pointed out that the state didn't need any particular forty, that the map was just to show the general idea. If somebody didn't want to sell his land, undoubtedly a neighbor nearby might be glad to do so. Nobody would be *forced* to sell his land.

There were farmers in that town hall who saw part of *their own land* crosshatched for purchase! Land had been condemned by the federal government in the nearby Necedah area, and farmers had been driven out—evacuated and moved elsewhere! "And now," they shouted, "it's going to happen here. Right here and to *us!*"

Frederick came home drained and exhausted. I had sense enough not to ask him how it went. After he finished eating his late supper in an absent-minded manner, he said so softly that I could hardly catch the words, "I thought they were going to tar and feather me." He tried to smile, "and run me out on a rail."

It was long, long ago, but that was the beginning of the worst year in my life. Of course some amusing things happened, but mighty few of them seemed funny at the time.

We continued to do our fieldwork on the marsh and were grateful when friends and neighbors waved to us or invited us in for a cup of coffee. Not everybody hated us. We also had sense enough to go to the local meetings and be seen.

The next time that Frederick had to go to one of those meetings in another town hall, it was PTA night and I had been invited. I telephoned ahead and said I was looking forward to coming. This was far from the truth. I was scared, but I wasn't going to let it show. A few minutes after I had put the receiver back on the hook, the telephone rang. "Mrs. Hamerstrom, we are *so* glad you are coming to PTA. We will have a debate." I caught my breath, for in my mind only one subject seemed up for debate right now. I could hardly believe what the principal was saying: "The debate will be on whether home economics should be taught in grade school or only at the high school level."

"Yes," I gasped.

"And we want you to be on one of the teams," he continued.

"Yes."

Frederick rummaged for his maps and set off for another town hall. I watched him get into the car and drive away, wishing with all my heart that I could go with him. My presence might keep the "party" from getting too rough.

I put on my best (and only) black dress, brushed my hair, and drove to Tri-County High in the truck—so steamed up about what might happen to Frederick that my memories of the debate are vague. The adrenalin pumping through my veins apparently caused me to put on an unusual performance. I pleaded the case on home economics with such passion that teachers and parents came up afterwards to congratulate me. In those days I was sure that home economics shouldn't be taught in school at all, and I have no idea which side I argued for. At any rate, the compliments buzzed about my astonished ears.

"Mrs. Hamerstrom, we had no idea you were such an eloquent speaker. We didn't know of your skill in forensics (I'd never debated before), and we want you for our president."

"President?"

"Yes, president of PTA."

I thanked them for the great honor and mumbled that it was really out of the question—working mother and that sort of thing.

I learned something very reassuring that evening. The Tri-County school, which was off the prairie chicken study area, was not out to get my skin. They seemed to be unaware of our troubles, and our children were not apt to suffer from their schoolmates as a result of the Prairie Chicken War. The size of the furor was limited, and the school lay outside of the battleground.

Cars in the drive

Frederick came back from the second mass meeting angry and bewildered. As far as I can recall this was the last meeting of this particular sort. Henceforth, for about a year, there were meetings right in our own house.

At about this time we bought Alan a dog and I took it to Wautoma, the county seat, for inoculations. I started home and decided to take the back roads for variety. The roads looked more and more unfamiliar, and soon I discovered that I was lost. The sun was still up and there was no possible excuse for getting lost. I stopped the car, studied the map and then—for the first time in many days—I took time to think. How could I, a professional biologist, lose my way within eighteen miles of home? I looked again at the setting sun. It gave me a clue, and I suddenly faced why I had gotten lost. It was psychological: I was *afraid* to go home.

Day after day the setting sun brought carloads of people into our driveway and into our house. For the most part they were loyal friends telling the new and often fabricated stories of what Mr. L. or somebody else had said or done toward running us out of the country. And they told us what our friends were saying: how Cecil Bender had stood right up to the town chairman, and that John Kraemer knew we were all right—he watched us at work in all weathers. Harry Chamberlain drove all over the marsh singing our praises and telling people what to think. He didn't stress competence or fairness. With deep rural wisdom he stressed two main points: these people wouldn't tell a lie—I know them—and they just love the prairie chickens.

We rarely had anything to contribute, but one evening Frederick electrified our friends by telling the story of the day. A farmer had stood right on his front steps in Coddington—a tiny town within our study area—and stated: "The government's going to flood the marsh and drive us all out. The south end is already under water and they are moving people out. Watch it: we come next."

The south end of the marsh was only ten miles from his house, but he had not bothered to look for himself. If he had, he would have found no water, no exodus, no change of any kind.

I tried to keep things reasonably normal for the children. When Alan and Elva came home on the school bus, I fed them and sometimes took them out to explore. But that left Frederick to cope with the excited babble of voices in our living room. We told both children exactly what was happening, so if they heard rumors or someone was nasty to them in school they would be armed with the same, pitiful morsels of information that we ourselves had. I'm convinced this was the right thing to do, although both children seemed to find our explanations rather boring. Elva occupied herself with a variety of pets and Alan asked me for a sheet.

"A sheet? What for?"

"I want a sheet. It doesn't have to be very good, but the top of the house is my pirate ship and I want to put up a flag."

Alan cut a skull and crossbones out of an old black dress and Mary Mattson sewed them on one of my old sheets. And in due time another story floated back to us: the Hamerstroms are spies. They are flying the flag of a foreign nation on top of their house. This was announced with much gusto, and then the teller of this particular tale lowered his voice and hissed in a sibilant whisper: "Must be *communists!*"

He passed this information on to the bluegrass crews. One of the major industries on the marsh was the harvesting of bluegrass seed. Machines known as "strippers" were pulled with tractors, and men rode the strippers. A rotating cylinder, covered with what appeared to be extruding nails, whirled the tops of ripe bluegrass into boxes or "hoppers." From time to time the tractor stopped, and the seed was unloaded into burlap bags. Now and again a young prairie chicken was whirled into the hopper along with the seed, but in general the bluegrass acreages were the heart of the prairie chicken area: vast expanses of land, managed to produce grass by periodic burning.

Needless to say, the bluegrass harvesters, who were known as strippers too, took sides in the Prairie Chicken War. Bluegrass seed is ripe for harvest about the first two weeks of July, when most of the young prairie chickens have hatched but can't fly very well yet. Frederick and Os and I went from crew to crew and asked each stripper to tell us how many broods he had seen and how big the chicks were. The three of us could have walked the marsh from dawn to dusk, day after day, and not gleaned as much information as we could get by simply asking the strippers.

I loved interviewing them, and whenever a stripper stopped, I used to unload his hopper so he could rest his aching muscles. At the end of the day the heavy bags had to be loaded onto trucks, and my muscles were easily up to hurling bags of seed up to the top of the load. Most of the strippers had milked cows early in the morning, finished their chores, and then put in some fourteen hours or so on the bouncing, clattering machines before going home to milk and finish up the evening chores.

The Prairie Chicken War altered our happy approach to the stripping crews. Some were so hostile that none of us liked to ask them about broods, and stories started flying: "Those prairie chicken people want to get rid of *us*. They saw a dead chick in my hopper."

We kept pointing out that a few dead chicks didn't matter a bit—that the seed industry was just wonderful for prairie chickens.

Not only did we have assembled cars in our driveway every evening but there were cars assembled around the taverns, and we well knew that we were among the chief subjects of conversation. As far as we knew, Frederick and Os were bearing the brunt of the talk and nobody had focused his attention on me. My time was to come.

Knitting on the street

And then, unexpectedly, we got a call from a professor at the university. I answered the telephone, but Professor V. said, "I'd rather speak with your husband." Odd way of putting it.

"Telephone!" I shouted, "and it's just for you!"

We hadn't had any trouble with the university, so I went back to mending equipment without feeling particularly uneasy. Frederick was at the telephone a long time, mostly listening, and when he finished I could see that he had bad news.

"What is it?" I asked.

For a moment I didn't think he was going to tell me. He just kept looking at me. Finally the words came. "They are talking about *you*."

"What are they saying?"

"He didn't want to tell me over the telephone. I told him we'd come right up."

I nodded slowly, and then getting on with the practical aspects, I said, "Let's dress up as though we were giving a lecture. It can't hurt to make a good impression."

Frederick changed into a suit and polished his shoes before putting them on. I put on my new beige stockings, a black dress, and high-heeled shoes. Then I fixed a quick cold supper for the children and left them a note:

We'll be back tonight.
Here is your supper.
Alan, please undo the buttons on the back of Elva's dress so she can get into her night clothes.

Frederick drove to Stevens Point with one hand so he could hold my hand with the other. They were talking about *me*, and I had given them so much to talk about: the flowers on the fence posts, planting the dead tree, or the sunny day I wore a raincoat. There were so many things that I felt steeped in guilt and didn't have sense enough to remind myself that I hadn't done anything really wrong— not as far as I knew.

When we got to the professor's house, Frederick brushed aside his greetings and said, "Well, what is it?"

Professor V. answered in a low voice, "The children aren't in bed. Won't you sit down?"

We seated ourselves uncomfortably on his big, soft sofa. He suggested that we should learn good public relations and help our neighbors with haying and barn-raising, but for the most part we discussed inconsequential matters while romping children managed to delay bedtime. At last Mrs. V. brought us some drinks and quietly left the room.

Frederick's voice was unsteady. He set his drink down untouched and, leaning toward the professor, he demanded, "What are they saying?"

The professor leaned forward and gave us the news. "They are saying," he paused, "that Mrs. Hamerstrom has been seen knitting on the street!"

"*Knitting?*" I asked.

"Yes," he nodded soberly. "*Knitting . . .* on the *street.*"

I looked up at him as though I were a little girl who had been caught doing something wrong and asked, "Is that so bad?"

Professor V. was surprised at the question.

At last he mumbled, "Why no, I suppose it isn't."

Mass hysteria plays queer tricks. Said in a certain deep tone, *seen knitting on the street* has an ominous ring, reminiscent of the sinister Madame Defarge and the French Revolution. Countless people, even a sensible professor who had tried to help us, were upset at this knitting business and failed to seek out the facts.

On the way home I laughed uncontrollably—without merriment—and then cowered against Frederick's arm and cried very softly. He probably preferred my little sobs to the wild laughter he had just been treated to.

Just about anyone in public service must have periods of great strain, but we weren't used to gossip and malice and we cared so much about saving the prairie chickens.

I still knit on the street. It's as good a place as any. And we won the Prairie Chicken War.

Years later I asked a neighbor, "Mary, remember when things were so bad and they had the mass meetings?"

She nodded.

"Why did people mind my knitting on the street?"

"Knitting on the *street?* You mean knitting on the road."

"On the road?"

"Ya. You'd go up on the marsh in the afternoon and park your car and knit—and taxpayers paying your salary!"

Mary patted my hand. "As for me, I figured it was nobody's business. You worked so hard and got up so awful early."

It was my turn to pat her hand. "I was working, Mary. I can knit without watching, and I had to wait to see what time the chickens came in to boom in the afternoon."

Mary gave a little snort of pleasure. "Now I've learned one thing and it's good.

"You learned the German way. It's the only way to knit—without watching your stitches."

The Hamerstrom rule of thirds

When we took our first pay job at the University of Michigan, Leopold chuckled and said, "You can satisfy the requirements in one third of your time." It was not at all plain to us what he meant, but perfectly plain that we were expected to do some thinking. We pondered this cryptic message and devised the Hamerstrom Rule of Thirds.

We never told our employers about the Rule of Thirds. It goes this way:

Spend one-third of your time on the mostly worthless red tape required by the administration.

Spend one-third of your time doing what is wanted of you, and what you want too.

Spend one-third of your time doing exactly what you please.

I am convinced that this formula is unbeatable. It is not for the lazy, but for those who are willing to put in the extra time—far beyond a 40-hour week—and the effort to earn that extra "free" third to do a first-rate job.

I really hadn't figured on entertaining 7,000 house guests, but this turned out to be the most electric part of the free third. It just happened that way so we could get the job done; it was never subsidized by the state.

Furthermore, if some nimble gentleman wanted to chase me all over the front yard trying to stuff a five dollar bill down the front of my shirt for the wonderful breakfast, I got his name and he got a receipt from the Prairie Chicken Foundation. We refused to take money. And a good thing too. If we had accepted money, our "guests" would have had a perfect right to complain that the mattresses were lumpy and the accommodations distinctly substandard.

154

I learned to be perfectly shameless about asking boomers to chip in food. Bill Pugh, one of the most outstanding friends of prairie chickens, who has done so much to save them, lives in Racine. Racine, Wisconsin, is the home of the kringle. The kringle is almost a coffee cake but so light and so alive with fruit and spices that it surpasses any Viennese pastry. Shamelessly, the Hamerstroms accepted kringles from Bill Pugh and his fabulously beautiful wife . . . and if Betty Pugh whispered, "These are just for you," we slipped the kringles out of sight very quickly so we could eat them alone.

We found that the aristocrats didn't grumble, and neither did the very rich, nor the very poor. Our rather few troubles came from some sort of stuffy in-between layer. That layer would come out with remarks like, "I can't imagine how the State of Wisconsin subsidizes *this!*"

This—the house, the breakfasts, the briefings, and the good fellowship was not what we were paid for. They were part of the third of our time that we had allotted to ourselves. I realize now that it was that extra "free" third that made it possible to save the prairie chickens.

The financial drain was not too bad because so many boomers brought coffee, eggs, bacon, and bread. But we never knew what might come in and had to keep the larder well stocked. The first time the Wisconsin Society for Ornithology scheduled a prairie chicken field trip, we failed to let Ed Peartree know that we couldn't guide an unlimited number of observers out to the blinds. Fourteen boomers stayed at our house, and nineteen more showed up unexpectedly for the First Breakfast at 2:30 A.M.! We knew they were coming, but not for breakfast! Each time one more walked in the back door I said, "Good morning," and broke two more eggs into a frying pan. I still remember a delightfully cultured voice asking, "Where do we warm the plates?"

I'm told I answered, "Oh, it's rather a warm morning." We served sixty-two eggs well before daybreak, and I was just hoping we had enough plates to put the eggs on.

After the booming season was over—seven days a week for eight to ten weeks—we sometimes just took off and went fishing with the children. Sometimes we took two or three days off without the slightest sense of guilt.

When we first started working for the Conservation Department about 1950, we were told, "A biologist's time is his own. He's expected to get the job done." Fair enough. Of course, we had to draw up work plans, keep track of official expenses, and write quarterly reports.

By the early 1970s great changes had come to pass. For one thing we were ordered to work *no more* than five days a week! To the best of my knowledge prairie chickens haven't the slightest idea what day of the week it is, and they boomed and fed energetically or not, depending on the weather. We solved that one by working in secret. We kept right on working seven days a week, but we had to cheat when reporting how many hours we worked each week.

This bothered us and was a far cry from "a biologist's time is his own." That was the union's doing.

In August of 1970 I got up early in the morning to work out some figures on population dynamics. Math is not my strong point, and I needed the cool early morning for concentration. By seven the household was moving, but I shut the door of my study and let everybody get his own breakfast.

At about 10:30 I finished running the calculator and had checked all my figures. I went over to the pond to take a break and swam slowly across the pond and back. Some of the men had left mist nets and poles on the beach. I picked up half of them to take them back and store them; then exhilarated by having finished complicated math and a nice swim, I picked up the rest and carried them toward the barn.

A strange little man in a business suit was more or less prancing around on our front lawn. I suspected he was a salesman of some sort.

"Are you Mrs. *Frances* Hamerstrom?"

I didn't like the way he said it. I was barefoot and wearing shirt and shorts, but I pulled myself up to my full height and said, "I'm *Doctor* Frances Hamerstrom."

I liked his next question even less. "Are you working?" He didn't say it nicely, like, "I wouldn't want to trouble you if you are working." The tone of the question was wrong.

I eased the poles off my shoulder—more poles than *he* could carry, I'm sure—and asked him, "Does it look it?"

"What are the poles for?" he persisted.

"These are mist net poles. The Department of Natural Resources in cooperation with the federal government is banding mourning doves. I'm storing equipment."

The little man wasn't going to let go. He said, "This is just a spot check."

I failed to grasp what he was saying; he sounded repulsively official.

156

"Would you like to see my supervisor?"

"Yes."

I showed him the way to Frederick's study. Frederick has enormous dignity. He told me afterwards, "That man was sent up from Madison to see if you were working. He was pretty sheepish."

It took me about five hours to absorb what had happened. The little man was long gone, but I wanted to shake him until his teeth rattled.

Of course it wasn't *his* fault. It was the fault of the system that sent out a snooper.

Drop nets and whipping cream

It has been said that essentially all the principles used by biologists for catching wild animals were known to Stone Age man, and it would not surprise me at all to learn that the drop net we used for catching prairie chickens had its prototype in the deepest of dark Africa where Pygmies netted elephants in eons past. But we learned of the drop net from Caleb Glazener, who used it for turkeys. It revolutionized our trapping. Bait piles of ear corn were pulled out onto the marsh by toboggan. Whenever a substantial flock of chickens took to feeding on a pile, we drove six steel fence posts into the frozen ground to support a forty- by forty-foot horizontal net. Few modern houses are forty-foot by forty. It was a big net. We did not use Stone Age materials. We bought fish netting, stretched it with steel fence posts and fastened it for quick release. Our pull wires, which sometimes were a quarter-mile long, came from the hardware store.

One man (or I) was hidden in a pit in the snow with nothing to do except give the pull wire a mighty heave when the signal came. Another (seldom me) had the task of deciding when the maximum number of chickens were under the net—decisions, decisions! I learned to avoid this.

Five chickens walking toward the net and three running out. Twenty six under at 3:15 and twenty under at 3:20, but seven rushing toward the net. I managed to get myself into that pit as often as possible. All the pit man had to do was pull the wire for all he was worth. Then six cotter pins slid through holes near the top of the fence posts, and the net dropped. The net bounded upwards once when the netted chickens tried to take off and then settled over the struggling chickens. We rushed in on snowshoes and hand-grabbed any birds that were likely to escape from the edges of the net.

Prairie chickens can entangle themselves in a net like Billy-be-damned in a matter of moments—after all, they are the wildest creatures I know. And I'd never known what to do with our children's outgrown socks; now I found a use. Each sock became a hood to slip over a bouncing chicken's head: a rubber band made it stay put. Once hooded, the cocks and hens behaved like ladies and gentlemen and ceased to struggle; then we could extricate them from the net without dislocated wings and other unmentionable horrors.

There was one hitch. Sometimes only five of the six cotter pins pulled loose. Part of the net remained tilted upwards, and most of the flock escaped.

The solution came from a most unlikely source. Dan Berger and Helmut Mueller, who were helping us then, tried various lubricants manufactured by the automotive industry, but even so and all too often, one corner of the net failed to fall.

One day I forgot to bring along any lubricant, and Mueller looked at me accusingly and said, "Fran, what have you got?"

I handed him my Tangee lipstick. It was the best lubricant of all.

HELMUT MUELLER AND FRAN

(Hugh Wilmar)

The press was attracted to our operations. Berger and Mueller had big black beards. I still remember a reporter from a Milwaukee paper, shivering in elegant field clothes. His pencil stopped moving when Berger ran over the bait pile and accosted Mueller. "Give me your lipstick!" Mueller reached in his pocket matter-of-factly and handed it over as the howling wind spat snow into our faces.

Not all our bait piles were near roads. Berger and I made one memorable set. We gunned the VW bus into the north end of the Buena Vista Marsh plunging through deep drifts. We both knew that if we could get the vehicle near the bait pile we could make a catch. The equipment for handling a big catch was more than we could carry, and there was no way that we could carry bags of chickens a mile or so to the bus without jeopardizing their lives.

How we were ever going to get the bus back onto a plowed road *after* the catch was a matter of secondary importance—simply a problem to be solved later. We shoveled through the drifts to get in, and our trail closed behind us in a smooth sweep of unbroken snow, masked by new falling snow and snow blown by the howling wind. At last we "parked" in sight of the net. We exposed the heap of corn under the net with a shovel and ran the long pull wire directly to the bus.

We waited snug in the bus with the set ready. Berger had a scope trained on the bait pile, and all I needed to do was to get out of the bus and give a mighty heave when he gave the signal. In the meantime I cooked dinner on the camp stove. It was Sunday: steak and potatoes; and strawberry shortcake for dessert.

The bus was like a little cave on an island—snug, resisting the wind, and isolated from the whole wide world. We ate our main course slowly, by which time the strawberries had thawed. Biscuits, left over from breakfast, were ready, and I sat on the floor in back of the bus to whip the rich, country cream we still could buy. Suddenly, without warning, I heard voices of strange men!

They were jackrabbit hunters and couldn't imagine why Berger was so happily relaxed inside a bus that was hopelessly stuck and far from any help.

We needed to get rid of those men. At any moment our chicken flock might swing by and be spooked by people in sight of the bait pile. I moved the eggbeater slowly, trying to think of what to say; I knew full well that if they ever realized we were doing something as fascinating as netting chickens they'd never go away.

Berger, who was sitting in the driver's seat, rolled down his window. The leader of the jackrabbit hunters said, "Young feller, you're stuck."

160

Berger answered easily, "We are not stuck. We're *parked*."

The hunter absorbed this amazing information slowly. Then it dawned on him that Berger had said *we*. He peered into the back of the bus and asked, "What's *she* doing?"

Berger answered a little impatiently. "You can see perfectly well what she's doing. She's whipping cream."

One by one the old men snowshoed to peer in the window nearest to me. I spun the eggbeater with enthusiasm as each wiped the window with his mitten and peered. Without another word they snowshoed away—off into the storm.

We made our catch within forty minutes and shoveled innumerable drifts getting the bus out to where Bill Peterson, the district ranger, could pull us onto a plowed road.

I never saw the three old men again. They missed watching the big drop net fall. They missed watching us band the chickens, and they missed sampling my strawberry shortcake topped with slightly overbeaten whipped cream.

The photographers

Photographers were always a special problem. Almost nobody (there were two exceptions) could take good notes and use a camera at the same time.

The old western saloons had a barrel by the door in which, on especially formal occasions, the customers were requested to leave their shooting irons. Frederick sometimes threatened to put a barrel by our back door, but for cameras.

Photographers tended to feel free to interrupt the briefing by asking at what speed they should shoot. Each detail of prairie chicken behavior described generated new enthusiasm for the equipment they had brought with them: long lenses, wide-angle lenses, special film, polarizing filters, etc.

Furthermore, with few exceptions, photographers are poor observers. So during the briefing we always asked, "Who brought a camera?"—just so we could put a good observer in the blind with him to take the notes. I know nothing about photography, nor do I intend to learn. What they say to each other is perfect gibberish to me, but there is no mistaking the tone of voice in which they speak to each other.

"I have a Ciné Special," one chap says eagerly.

"Oh!" the other replies, "that's a nice little camera. I had one years ago."

And then at the Second Breakfast they have a go at it again.

"How many feet did you shoot?"

"Four rolls."

"Did you *really*? The light was so bad today that I didn't even take my camera out of its case, but maybe you got something. . . ."

Photographers have taken knives and cut huge camera ports in the sides of our carefully constructed blinds.

It is the photographers who often have so much to carry that

162

they want a biologist to tote some of their gear for them! And some of them have simply moved our blinds to suit mysterious purposes of their own: backlighting, for example. But their chief complaint was usually about the inappropriate height of the windows in the blinds.

Many photographers, of course, are wonderful people and we are grateful for the pictures and films they have given us, but a certain wariness creeps over me every time I see a camera.

One morning at the Second Breakfast, Henry, a portly, somewhat elderly duck hunter and his wife Mabel bubbled with enthusiasm for the prairie chickens, but asked me, "Why are the windows in the blind so low?"

"Low? Are you photographers?"

"No, we were just watching." Mabel added, "We took turns watching."

"You took *turns?* Why?" This whole business of the low windows was becoming more and more mystifying.

"There wasn't room for both of us to look out of the windows at once."

"We've never heard of a complaint like this before. Those windows are at eye level and every blind has six windows."

"Yes," she answered, "but our eyes were so low down. We had to take turns on our hands and knees." These dear old people smiled at each other understandingly. She explained, "We are both so very plump."

I got to liking them more and more, but I couldn't imagine what on earth they were talking about. "Why didn't you just get in the blind and sit on the bench?"

"The bench?" she asked and added, "Why Henry, there *was* a bench. A nice little bench right out among the birds!"

In a dizzying moment their predicament became clear to me. Yesterday's wind had capsized their blind and blown it away from the bench as well. They had spent the morning in an upside-down blind!

Tail end of spring

Morning! The pale glint of pre-dawn outside our bedroom window outlines the barn and I get up running. It must be that the alarm clock has failed because Frederick, who usually gets up first, is still asleep. I stand baffled in the kitchen. No eggs counted out . . . no plates ready . . . no clutter of gear on the floor.

No boomers. The season is over and the perpetual houseparty is past until another year.

The old house is very quiet.

AFTER BOOMING SEASON, THE BRIEFING ROOM BECAME MY STUDY AGAIN.

Pavlov conditioned dogs to salivate when they heard the dinner bell. I have been conditioned too. My internal clock is set for pre-dawn in spring. (It's ten years since our last boomers have come and gone, and I still wake up from time to time ready to run, to cook, to guide to the blinds.)

BOOMERS WERE SOMETIMES DISCOURAGED FROM ENTERING FREDERICK'S STUDY BY LEAVING THE LIGHTS OFF. . . . AND THE CURTAINS OF FISHNETTING WERE OFTEN DRAWN TO EXCLUDE OWLS

Every spring I was conditioned anew to the heady excitement of laughter, of strangers in the house—the fascinating mishmash of volunteers from all walks of life; then—not unmixed with relief that another season had gone well—there was always a sense of loss when it was all over.

THE SAME OVAL MIRROR HANGS ON ANOTHER WALL OVER THE SAME BLUE SOFA AS IT DID 45 YEARS AGO WHEN I WAS SO UNCERTAIN AND YOUNG

It would be exhilarating to hear, just once more, the cars of the boomers pull into the drive, give a briefing, and get everybody out to the blinds before the cold gray dawn. . . .

166

But at the end of each booming season we had more time for the children. Time to field tough questions like, "Why is the sky?" or, "If an owl saw me pushing a baby buggy would it be surprised?"

I cannot imagine what it must have been like to be brought up a Hamerstrom child. We brought them up under rules—or better still, policies. The first, established the day Alan was born, was:

> We do not own our children
> Our children own themselves

This meant that even as toddlers they were treated with the same courtesy as grownups. Mind you, one does lose one's temper from time to time—and then apologizes.

Our second policy was: always say *yes* when you possibly can; only say *no* when you have to. When Alan asked, "Can I go barefoot in the snow?" I absentmindedly corrected his English and answered, "You *may*."

In 1954 we were invited to go to Finland—a chance to study grouse in the far North. We held a family council. "You Alan, will go to a horseback riding camp in Arizona."

Alan's answer was a shout. "Hi . . . yo . . . Silver!"

"And Elva will go to visit her grandmother."

"I don't want to. I want to stay here and look after my pets."

Frederick shook his head, and I added, "You are only eleven; we can't let you spend the night alone in this house."

Drear rain beat against the windows as Elva slowly left the room—I supposed to take comfort from one of her many pets. I knew no way to console her so I left her alone.

About forty minutes later she burst into the house, drenched by the downpour which was getting heavier. "I fixed it! Mrs. Jorgenson says that Nancy and I can spend the nights in their old chicken coop. We're going to fix it up for a clubhouse."

Frederick and I looked at each other. "You mean," he asked, "you plan to spend the *days* here and the *nights* at the Jorgensons?"

"Sure. I have my bicycle and it's only half a mile."

(Always say *yes* when you possibly can.)

We said yes.

Perhaps because we were a mite worried about this unconventional arrangement, we told the sheriff that the house would be empty for a couple of months and asked him to stop in now and again.

True to his word, he stopped, and when we came back his story ran something like this:

"The driveway hadn't been used for a long time. The door was wide open. I knocked; nobody came so I walked in. A white chicken squawked and jumped off a sofa, and a rabbit hopped out of another room like he was waiting for me.

"Then I opened a door and a big owl, sitting on the back of a chair, bobbed its head like it was going to come for me. I shut that door quick and went upstairs.

"None of the beds had been slept in; some kid had left crayon drawings of animals on one of them. Back in the kitchen I could smell somebody had been cooking, and there was fresh food in the refrigerator.

"I went outside to think. There were bicycle tracks in the drive. I'd missed them before. Then I heard sounds I couldn't figure out at all . . . way out back of a big plum thicket.

"I moseyed over and there was a pretty little girl, sitting in a patch of daisies, playing a clarinet.

"I didn't want to scare her, so I waited till she saw me. I asked her, 'Where are your parents?'

"That little kid smiled at me. Guess what she said?

'I don't know. I think they're in Lapland.' "*

---

* This seemingly permissive upbringing did not quench the independent spirit of our offspring. Neither followed in our footsteps. Elva—true to the crayon drawings of her pets—is now a wildlife artist; and Alan—perhaps true to his Viking ancestors—is a yacht broker.

Let me sew her up

Frederick pulled another prairie chicken out of one of the bouncing, wailing bags in the tiny blind. "She's gangrenous," he said. "What a mess. I'll kill her."

"Give her to me." I grabbed the hen by both legs, immobilized her wings between my knees, and examined the wound. Torn skin exposing the flesh beneath ran along her slim pulsing neck, across her barred breast, down across her belly, and just missed her hip joint.

It was February. The northwest wind tore at the small window slots of our four-foot-square blind; now and again puffs of snow seeped in to dust us and the wounded prairie hen. Instinctively, I shifted her position to protect the exposed wound from wind and snow.

"Must have hit a fence." Frederick reached for the bird. "Give her to me."

I shook my head. "Let me sew her up. It will take just a minute."

Side by side we sat on a wooden bench three feet long and nine inches wide. We argued. Seed pearls of sparkling frost clung to Frederick's black mustache, and my fingers—tight around the chicken's legs—pulled pain deep into my mittenless hand.

Behind us, in gunnysacks, the chickens we had already caught wailed and mewed their complaint. Suddenly one fluttered. One wing beat was enough to set off the chain reaction. Two bags of birds leapt as though possessed by seventeen devils of hell, and every chicken in those bags lost precious energy before release time.

Frederick gave me *the look*.

Just then a little bit of gray knitted wool—the spare sock—beckoned to me. It was wedged under his end of our bench. It's hard enough for somebody six foot one and in full winter regalia to get up from a tippy bench just nine inches high—and even harder when the roof is only four inches above his head.

"Could you lift your end of the bench just a little?"

Silence.

Frederick is not only my husband but also my boss; I am his assistant and get a lesser salary. He has a perfect right to order me about. He doesn't: he just tells me what to do in a reasonable tone of voice.

No houses in sight. We two alone out on the marsh. White-out of snow. *One* gray sock was all that I wanted.

Taking a leaf from Frederick's book, I inquired in an offhand, reasonable tone of voice, "Why don't you lift up your end of the bench so we can start processing?"

My eyes were on the sock, so I didn't see his face. Perhaps, if I had glanced at it, I would not have pursued the matter. Slowly he eased one boot around the end of the bench, shifted his weight carefully, and pulled upwards. My muscles were primed to get my weight off that bench and reach for the sock in perfect timing with his effort. But, handicapped by the chicken between my knees, my foot slipped and I sat down with a thump.

The wailing of the prairie chickens was punctuated by a low grunt from the throat of my man.

"Sorry," I mumbled.

With a degree of instant nimbleness that I managed to muster against almost impossible odds in that cramped space, I half slid, half bounced off my end of the bench and knelt in the snow.

Frederick moved his heavy boot once more, shifted his weight carefully, and eased his end of the bench up an inch or two, and I wrenched the sock out with a mighty jerk.

Then I pushed the hen down into the sock where she would rest in her gentle straitjacket.

Meekly, I asked, "Would you like me to help you set up the scales?" Silly question: of course we were going to set up the scales and weigh and band and process and release those bags full of chickens. But I couldn't think of anything else to say at the moment. "Thank you" would have been a mite inadequate, and for once "thank you" lacked tact.

Frederick set up the scales. I untied one bag and felt carefully deep down into the warm feathery interior. I felt for both legs of *one* chicken and managed to pull a bird out of the bag without setting the rest aflutter. It took a steady hand and a good deal of practice; I was going to see to it that the model wife and perfect assistant was doing her work without blunders.

We love working together and it isn't often that the little clash of wills interrupts our teamwork. For the next half-hour or so we weighed and processed one bird after another. It became a smooth routine. Weigh, process, band, and peek out of the window to check the traps; then push the bird out of the little window for release.

Suddenly, Frederick whispered, "Chickens." A flock of about thirty came swinging in from the west, flutter-braked, and landed at the edge of the cornfield. They started walking toward our well-baited traps.

"Do we have some empty bags?"

Frederick nodded. From now on we would put processed chickens into empty bags for we had no intention of frightening the flock away by letting even one clattering chicken emerge from the window—our usual method of release.

From time to time I peeked at my patient. Her feathered feet with their delicate snowshoes—those little combs on each toe—remained upright and motionless. Would she ever run again? Would she ever fly?

At last our catch was processed and ready for release. Some of the traps seemed blackened with birds. Frederick peered out of his window. "We've got all we can handle. Let's go."

We tipped the blind, which had no door, over on its side. The late afternoon light dazzled our eyes, and fresh outdoor cold stung our cheeks and our noses. We released the processed birds, put on our snowshoes, and mushed out to the traps to bring in our second catch.

I said, "Darling, this is crazy. What made you think of working out of a blind here instead of running the trapline?"

Frederick was balancing the scales again . . . "Just had a hunch today." His hunch had been good. We two were sitting in a blind chalking up a record catch.

Again we processed and released, and I produced two almond Hershey bars out of my inside shirt pocket when it was really time for us to be on our way home.

We munched. It was a good moment. Our bones ached and the cold had taken its toll on us. A mackerel sky, laced with orange and purple, promised another big catch for the morrow.

Frederick said, "It was a good day." And I could follow his thinking: a record catch, and nothing to do but snowshoe to the car with the scales and equipment, *start* the car, push home through the drifts, and enter a stone-cold house where he would get the fire going and I would cook a good supper.

Instead I said, "Darling, please pass me the needle and thread."

Frederick said, "What?"

"The light is getting very bad and I need to sew her up now."

"Her?"

"You remember—that hen that I socked."

My man can mesmerize a prairie chicken. He held that bird while I sewed her up. Even in the bitter cold we both could detect the stench of putrifying flesh and, in the less than half-light, the green of gangrene loomed ominously. His long, clever fingers manipulated the bird. I loosened the skin along the whole length of the wound, and then I pulled gently to find the *middle* of the tear in the skin . . . not the middle by math, the middle by feel. Having found my intangible middle, my fingers found new "middles"—not true middles, because my fingers had to allow for the unseemly stretchable skin of the neck and belly. I used cotton thread and an ordinary sewing needle, tying the square knots quickly and then holding up the threads for Frederick to clip my sutures.

We processed her. She weighed 726.2 grams and the bands she wore were green 23 over red. When we released her, she flew—away into the deep, dark dusk. She *flew*.

We headed home, and after we got the stove going in the kitchen, we had mulligan for supper. Then we crawled into bed. I whispered, "I'm sorry. I was pretty silly about that hen."

"What?"

"I was pretty silly about that hen today."

Frederick's only answer was, "I was *asleep!*"

That dratted hen had whizzed off into the night from the south end of the Buena Vista Marsh and I wished her well. Would she had wished me the same!

On April 28, the following spring, I came back from watching displaying prairie chickens from a blind and announced with much excitement, "I saw a hen with a brood patch!"

"Brood patch!" Frederick exclaimed with interest. "We've never seen a hen with a brood patch on a booming ground. We've been quite certain that one copulation is enough to fertilize a whole clutch of eggs." A brood patch—a big bare patch on the belly— implied that a prairie hen had started incubation and was coming back for another insemination.

"I saw it. Her belly feathers were every which way. And right where the brood patch has got to be!"

Frederick is a patient man. "Did you get her bands?"

"Yes, green 23 over red."

He walked over to the files and looked up the number. Then he looked at me with astonishment. "That was the gangrenous hen at Skrznecki's. She lived, but I don't think what you saw was a brood patch. It looks as though you didn't sew her belly up just right."

Ought to be the end of that hen's story, but no. I told it more than once—amusing story—and became quite a heroine for saving that bird's life. But year after year I watched the range of our prairie chickens disappear under the plow and drainage. And I began to grow up. I came to realize that the saving of one individual for sentimental reasons is nothing compared to preservation of habitat for a species.

Frederick knew this all the time.

An introduction

Once when we were lecturing in Europe, we were introduced by Karl von Frisch (who later won the Nobel Prize for his work on bees).

After cake and coffee served in an arbor in his garden, where it seemed to me the conversation was pleasant but idle, we soon found ourselves in one of the biggest lecture halls we'd ever been in. And we soon learned that conversation in the arbor had not been idle. Von Frisch smiled at us in a kindly way and addressed the audience.

"Sometimes it comes to pass that a young man shows a marked interest in natural history, pursues his interest assiduously, and has a distinguished career."

I wanted to squeeze Frederick's hand, but we were sitting in the front row and the atmosphere was formal.

Von Frisch continued. "Sometimes it comes to pass that a young woman shows a marked interest in natural history, pursues her interest assiduously, and has a distinguished career." I was beginning to feel uncomfortable. It seemed the professor was laying it on a bit thick. He raised both hands palms upward. "And sometimes, but far more rarely, it comes to pass that two such young people meet as a result of their common interest in natural history, and pursue their interest with diligence together and—as a result—have distinguished careers.

"I take great pleasure in introducing Doctors Frederick and Frances Hamerstrom." Von Frisch paused dramatically. "With them it was not the case. She fell in love with him because he dances so beautifully."